Collins

need to know?

Karate

Lloyd Bradley

Collins

First published in 2007 by Collins
an imprint of
HarperCollins Publishers
77–85 Fulham Palace Road
London w6 8JB

www.collins.co.uk

Collins is a registered trademark of
HarperCollins Publishers Limited

10 09 08 07
6 5 4 3 2 1

A catalogue record for this book is available from
the British Library

Produced for Collins by Essential Works Ltd
168a Camden Street, London NW1 9PT
www.essentialworks.co.uk
For Essential Works:
Editor: Barbara Dixon
Designer: Kate Ward
Photographer: Gary Ombler

Series design: Mark Thomson
Front cover photograph: © jupiterimages
Back cover photographs, from left to right:
Stockbyte Platinum/Alamy; Medio Images/Corbis;
Pixland/Corbis

ISBN-13: 978-0-00-723404-2
ISBN-10: 0-00-723404-x

Printed and bound by Printing Express Ltd,
Hong Kong

**Essex County
Council Libraries**

Contents

Introduction

There probably aren't as many reasons for wanting to learn karate – sport ... self-defence ... keep fit ... spirituality – as there are styles of karate to learn, but whatever your motivation there is a style and approach for you. As you begin to learn, however, you will come up against not only the multitude of types of martial art – karate, kung fu, tae kwon do, aikido and so on – but also the numerous styles within each type. Then there'll be such questions as how do I find a good club to join? What equipment will I have to buy? Is it very difficult? How do I avoid injury?

Initially, this book aims to answer the big question 'Which style of martial art?' by focusing on Japanese karate, then detailing the basic kicks and punches relevant to its four most popular sub-styles. We will then take you through subjects such as the history of karate; why the *dojo* (training hall) is a special place with its own set of rules; how to buy and care for your *gi* (karate suit); and how to prepare to train to avoid common injuries. The book also offers advice on choosing a karate club and what steps you should next take to progress as a *karateka* (student).

In short, we aim to give you a good enough grounding in the techniques and philosophies of karate to convince you that it will be worthwhile carrying on and joining a club. That will be where you can build on what the book has taught you, and you will have a definite advantage as you start to progress through the rankings.

1 What is karate?

Karate is a martial art, but with the emphasis on the 'art' as much as the 'martial'. The *karateka*, or student, will learn not only effective self-defence and fighting techniques, but also balance, grace, self-control, concentration and self-awareness. Karate is also excellent for keeping fit, and teaches team spirit and consideration, since in any good karate club, or *dojo*, there is mutual respect and a sense of camaraderie. This section introduces the history and philosophy of karate, preparing you for the first steps of the journey to *karate-do*, the way of the empty hand.

The history of karate

There are records of martial arts being practised in China as long ago as the 12th century BC, but the history and popular development of karate in Japan is much more modern.

The secret art

The term karate comes from the synthesis of two Japanese words: *kara* meaning empty and *te* meaning hand, and was first formalized and popularized in Japan as late as the 1920s. From this time karate could be taught and learned openly. For centuries prior to this, the Japanese authorities had banned any form of martial art for fear of a people's revolution. It was this need for secrecy that

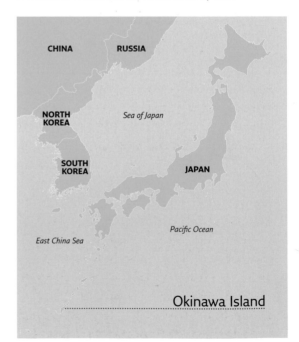

Martial arts originated in China, were taken to Okinawa and from there to mainland Japan.

contributed greatly to how and why the art developed in Japan. Karate was first practised in Japan on the small, nominally independent island of Okinawa, where, as one of the country's southern-most islands, there was a large Chinese and Korean influence from its neighbours. Since the 12th century Okinawa's ruling classes had travelled to China to be formally taught martial arts, while as trade between the island and the Chinese mainland flourished the rest of the population learned combat techniques from travellers and visitors.

In the 1600s the Satsumas (a fierce Japanese clan) took over Okinawa and to discourage revolt banned the practice of martial art and confiscated all weapons. Resistance to these new rulers took the form of underground karate practice, during which the 'empty hand' fighting style evolved as something far more direct and less flamboyant than much of

This garden in Okinawa provides space for meditation and contemplation, which was also provided in the original *dojos*.

the kung fu imported from China. Farm implements such as rice flails, staffs and sickles were pressed into service as weapons, creating a series of techniques that remain in place today. Because of the clandestine nature of karate training, there wasn't much movement or exchange of ideas around the island and three distinct variations of style evolved: Shuri-te, Tomari-te and Naha-te, each named after the city from which it emerged. It is these styles that are credited with evolving into modern Japanese karate.

Karate remained underground as the peasants' form of resistance, until the Satsumas were overthrown at the end of the 19th century and martial arts came out of the shadows. At the beginning of the 20th century karate became part of the Okinawan schools programme, introduced by Master Anko Itosu and readily accepted as part of post-feudal Japan's increasing militarism. Itosu is widely acknowledged as the father of modern Japanese karate, since the techniques he developed, particularly in the teaching of beginners, remain as the basis of all the main styles.

As a martial art – rather than strictly a combat method – karate made its official entrance on the Japanese mainland in 1922, when the Master Gichin Funakoshi (see box), gave a demonstration at a major sporting exhibition in Tokyo. Funakoshi was an Okinawan who had studied under Itosu, and such was the demand for his teaching that he settled on the mainland. Japan took to karate with gusto: it was taught at schools and colleges, in government offices, youth groups, the armed forces, factories and businesses. During the following decade many Okinawan karate masters relocated to the mainland.

did you know?

Although it is rarely documented, women and children also practised karate in the early days. Indeed there were many Chinese and Japanese princesses skilled in martial arts, and they contributed hugely to its development.

Among them were Hironori Ohtsuka, Chojun Miyagi and Kenwa Mabuni who, respectively, developed the styles of Wado-ryu, Goju-ryu and Shito-ryu, which along with Funakoshi's Shotokan, established the four main styles of Japanese karate. At this time, too, karate developed into a bona fide sport, emphasis shifting from technique and *kata* (form) to incorporate much more free sparring and competition events.

The spread of karate across the rest of the world came about during the late 1940s and 1950s for two reasons. During the American occupation of Japan in the Second World War many US servicemen learned karate and took it home with them. Then, after the war had devastated the Japanese economy and way of life, many from that nation moved abroad and they too took karate with them.

Today, in its many variations, karate is practised all over the world, as much a part of international sporting culture as boxing or wrestling.

Karate Masters, from left to right: Toyama Kanken, Hironori Ohtsuka, Shimoda Takeshi, Funakoshi Gichin, Motobu Choki, Kenwa Mabuni, Nakasone Genwa and Taira Shinken.

The *dojo*

Translated into English, *dojo* simply means 'the place of the Way' and the word will be applied to any formal karate training space. In the UK, where there are very few dedicated karate training halls, a *dojo* might be a church hall, a space in a leisure centre, part of a gymnasium, or even a room above a pub.

must know

When visiting a *dojo*, even if you have not joined the club or are not yet undergoing karate training, please try to observe *dojo* etiquette – if for no other reason than to create a good impression.

Entering the Way

However, for those who use it, the *dojo* will always be much more than the building alone. *Dojos* are symbolic of karate itself, and by entering the *dojo* you are giving yourself over to be part of the art; therefore you must respect the space itself as being a portal into 'the Way'. On entering or leaving bow to the *dojo* as a mark of respect. The *dojo* is a place of enormous discipline, self-control, respect for the instructor and fellow students and is, seemingly, surrounded by a great number of rules.

In fact, when you enter a correctly run *dojo* from the bustle of the outside world, you will experience a truly unique atmosphere.

The rules and codes of conduct are there for good reason: a calm atmosphere, free from distractions, will help you to get the best out of your training session. Karate sparring and practice could be very dangerous if you aren't paying attention. The spiritual aspect of being part of the *dojo* goes a long way to instilling in students the notion of karate as a way of life rather than just a martial art, while the idea that you have entered something bigger than yourself keeps students humble even after they've gained their black belt (see page 180).

Ten rules of *dojo* etiquette

1 Bow to the *dojo* on entering or leaving.

2 Remove shoes before entering the *dojo*.

3 If class is already in session when you arrive, wait at the back of the *dojo* until called forward.

4 Do not walk in between *sensei* (teacher) and class; cross the *dojo* around the back of students.

5 Do not talk in class.

6 Ask questions at prescribed times only – unless it is a genuine emergency.

7 Keep the *dojo* clean and tidy.

8 Respect other students – bow to each other when paired up; be careful when sparring.

9 Food and drink are not allowed in the *dojo*, except for water by permission of the *sensei*.

10 Always try your hardest. This is out of respect for the *dojo*, your *sensei* and your fellow students.

Karate students and master in the *dojo*.

Different styles of karate

There are many different styles of karate, but only four are widely practised, and although the same basic approaches apply to each, the further you get into any of them the more unique you will find each to be.

did you know?

Elvis Presley studied Shotokan karate during his time in Germany in the US Army. The karate moves he incorporated into his later stage shows were based on Shotokan *katas* (see box opposite).

The four main styles

There are over 30 acknowledged schools or styles of karate practised throughout the world, and although to the beginner many may not seem to differ too much, each will have its own approaches and techniques.

However, both in Japan and in the West, there are really only four styles that are at all widespread – Shotokan, Goju-ryu, Shito-ryu and Wado-ryu. Other popular styles are Kyokushinkai, Shudokan and Shorinji Kempo, but if you join a karate club in the UK the chances are it will teach one of the four former styles.

Shotokan (*show*-toe-karn)

The name literally means 'The House of Waving Pines', and this is probably the most widely practised form of karate. Shotokan was developed by Gichin Funakoshi, the man credited with introducing karate to the Japanese mainland at the beginning of the 20th century, and the name is derived from his *dojo*, which combined the pen name he used as a poet – Shoto, meaning waving pines – and kan, meaning house of. It is widely perceived to be the more universal method, since Funakoshi's intent was to unite and simplify two Japanese styles that he had been studying: Shorei and Shorin. By fusing together elements of two styles, Shotokan combines the power of the former with the flexibility of movement of the latter, yet distils it into very straightforward techniques. Although advanced students will move freely and obliquely during *kata* and sparring, Shotokan's essentially straightforward technique involves powerful linear approaches and attacks delivered from solid, deep stances. It is a popular competition style.

Goju-ryu (*godg*-oor-roo)

Quite literally, the hard/soft style – 'go' translates as 'hard' and 'ju' as 'soft', with 'ryu' meaning 'school' – this technique involves meeting hard with soft and vice versa, since practitioners will counter hard punches and kicks with soft, deflective blocking, or strike a soft heel of the hand against a hard head, or attack a soft groin with a hard foot. The idea is that such a technique is more energy efficient and ultimately effective than meeting force with force. Goju-ryu has many movements in its repertoire and combines direct linear attacking with circular and oblique movements. The style is not really considered a sports or competition style, but a powerful method of self-defence.

Goju-ryu is derived from one of the four original karate styles from Okinawa, where it was developed by Chojun Miyagi in the first half of the 20th century, after he had studied in Naha for many years. It has remained virtually unchanged since it began. This is largely due to the fact that it has been passed down through three generations of *karateka* within the same *dojo*.

must know
A *kata* is a sequence of karate movements done without an opponent.

The *katas* in this book are based on Shotokan, which is probably the most appropriate style for children learning karate, as it is the most straightforward.

However, all styles of karate are essentially the same as regards the basic movements for beginners.

Shito-ryu (*shee*-toe-roo)

A style predominant in Western Japan, Shito-ryu was founded in the 1920s by Kenwa Mabuni as a combination of the Naha-te and Shuri-te styles – the name is actually a combination of part of the name of each of Mabuni's teachers.

The style is characterized by its low, short-based stances, more often square-on than side-on, from which sharp, linear attacks are launched with an emphasis on explosive power. Shito-ryu has around 50 *katas* – more than any of the other Big Four styles, and prospective black belts will have to study two dozen, but it is also a style that requires success at competition sparring to progress through the rankings. Traditional Japanese weapons such as the staff and *nunchaku* (two sticks connected at their ends with a short chain or rope) will be introduced to higher grades of Shito-ryu students.

Wado-ryu (*Wad*-oh-roo)

Wado-ryu translates as 'The Way of Peace or Harmony', and the style is far less directly aggressive than the above, with an emphasis on evasive technique. It was founded in 1932 by Hironori Ohtsuka, a former assistant to Gichin Funakoshi, as a style that was based upon a spiritual inner calm rather than expert kicks and punches. As a result, Wado-ryu is a fluid, perpetually body-shifting style developed with a main aim to avoid attack and retaliate as concisely as possible with sharp, usually close-up attacks. During Wado-ryu training a relatively large amount of time will be devoted to self-control, spiritual development, respect for others and humility.

did you know?

Cinema idols Bruce Lee, Jackie Chan and Jet Li all practised Chinese Kung fu, although in Bruce Lee's case he also became a master of several different Japanese styles.

Kung fu and Tae kwon do (*Tie*-kwon-doh)

Kung fu translated means 'achievement through great effort' and it is the catch-all Western term for Chinese martial arts, whatever the style – and there are many, many different styles. The term didn't come into popular use until the mid-20th century, and is not found in Chinese texts dating back from before the 1800s.

Martial arts have been recorded as being practised in China since the 12th century BC, and although the aims are the same – empty hand combat – the repertoire of movements, strikes and forms are, for the most part, far more varied and elaborate than in Japanese karate.

Tae kwon do is Korea's national sport and the modern style has developed as a combination of Chinese and Japanese martial arts and traditional Korean methods. Tae kwon do is a very aggressive, straightforward and mobile style relying on attack as the best form of defence and powerful kicks being the best form of attack, since they will keep the opponent at bay. Due to its popularity in the USA, the style is the most widely practised martial art in the West, and became an official, full-fledged Olympic sport at the 2000 Olympic Games in Sydney.

Although many of the basic movements, kicks and punches in Japanese, Chinese and Korean martial arts may appear to be the same, they should not be confused with each other. There will be numerous subtle differences in how they are actually performed, as well as enormous variations of application. The differences will be most apparent in *katas* and sparring situations.

want to know more?
• This book is devoted to Japanese karate, to find out more about Chinese Kung Fu or Korean Tae kwon do, we recommend the following books:
Simply Wing Chun Kung Fu by Ip Chun
(The Crowood Press)
The State of the Art Tae kwon do by Master Sung Chul Whang and Master Jun Chul Whang
(Broadway Books).

websites
• British National Martial Arts Association:
www.bnmaa.co.uk
• British TaekwonDo Council:
www.britishtaekwondocouncil.org
• British Kung Fu Association:
www.laugar-kungfu.com

2 Getting started

Before you throw a punch or execute a kick, there is a great deal a beginner needs to consider – from what style would suit you best and what equipment you'll need to buy, to how to behave in a *dojo*. It is all part of becoming a *karateka* and you should approach these aspects thoughtfully and with full understanding. In this section we will provide you with an insight into every new student's basic preparations.

The best style for you

A question frequently asked by those about to start learning karate is 'Which style is best?' The simple answer is that none of them is better than any of the others; each has its own advantages, disadvantages and peculiarities.

must know

Although choosing a style may be fairly theoretical, choosing a club is very different; there will be good and bad clubs offering every style. Don't be tempted to 'make allowances' for a club you're not 100 per cent happy with just because it teaches your style of choice.

Your objective

At this stage, choosing the right club (see page 176) is going to be a far more important consideration than choosing a style. However, there are a few basics to consider before you run up against the bewildering number of systems and clubs on offer when you log on to sortmeoutakarateclub.com or something very similar. It all depends on why you've opted to learn karate in the first place and what you want to get out of it.

You want to be the next Bruce Lee

That probably won't happen! The styles learnt by Bruce Lee and Jackie Chan and seen in most of the movies is Chinese kung fu and it does seem to have the most screen-friendly moves, but it is also very spiritual and you will need a lot of patience and inner calm to get to a point at which you are performing almost as spectacularly. As far as karate goes, Shito-ryu will probably suit you best, since it has an emphasis on tournament fighting and incorporates weaponry.

You want to fight in competitions

Once again, Shito-ryu, with its emphasis on sparring, will suit you, as will Shotokan, simply because there are so many Shotokan clubs and thus there are a great number of competitions and tournaments.

You want to learn self-defence

For women, because a male attacker is likely to be stronger and heavier, a martial art such as judo or jiu jitsu, which uses the opponent's weight and strength against them, is one of the more realistic options. But karate does appeal to many women. When choosing a club or class, Wado-ryu, which is built on evasive techniques and sharp counter-attacks, would be best. Or Goju-ryu, which does not rely on meeting force with force, making it more effective for those with less physical strength.

You want to get fit

All karate training should get you fit, but the best style for that specific purpose would be Shotokan, with its combination of power and flexibility that will work your body in a way that is best for it.

You are looking for the spiritual side

Once again, every good karate teacher ought to be emphasizing the contemplative nature of karate training and the inner calm it can produce, but of the 'Big Four' Japanese styles, Wado-ryu has the greatest spiritual aspect.

Learning a martial art will boost your confidence.

---

must know

When you visit a club you are thinking about joining, talk to the instructor about your reasons for wanting to learn karate. He or she will be happy to do this.

Karate kit

Because of its origins and philosophy, karate is essentially an uncomplicated martial art, available to all whatever their circumstances, and thus there is not much special equipment needed to practise it. However, what kit there is has to be treated with respect.

The gi

The karate *gi* (suit) is an instantly recognizable 'uniform' of the martial artist and the only compulsory piece of equipment in many traditionally run *dojos*. For these reasons it is taken very seriously as the badge of the *karateka*.

The white, baggy, pyjama-style clothing is very practical, since it is non-constrictive, relatively light, cool and with no zips or metal fastenings to injure yourself or an opponent; but it also has meaning within karate's spiritual side. Everybody in a class will be dressed the same, symbolizing their essential equality; the pristine white of your *gi* should be a mark of the purity of spirit of the *karateka*, while it also represents a blank canvas to show that everybody still has much to learn.

The *gi*'s trousers will tie with a drawstring waist and the double-breasted jacket fastens with a tie at each side.

Choosing a gi

Many clubs will sell *gis* to new students, often at a reduced rate, and if this option is open to you it is recommended for more reasons than just the saving – your instructor is not likely to want a class full of shabby-looking students, so it will probably be of good quality; what profit there is goes to your club and not to a shop; you will be able to see similar *gis* of various vintages on existing students, and so get a good idea of how it will wear. And if it does turn out to be shoddy, you can easily take it back!

If you are buying a new *gi*, visit a reputable sporting goods or karate equipment dealer, try it on and ensure you can move freely in it, then ask about potential shrinkage. Inexpensive isn't always the best value, since if you are going to take your karate seriously, training sessions involve a great deal of potentially wearing floor work and the frequent washing and ironing will take its toll. Often, the more robust fabric of heavier suits will be a better choice.

Care of your *gi*

A clean, wrinkle-free *gi* is mandatory in most well run *dojos*, thus it must be washed and ironed before every session. If your training programme and your everyday schedule do not allow for this, you will need more than one *gi*. Any repairs on rips or split seams must be carried out before the next session, as these could prove dangerous during sparring.

Badges

Clubs will often have their own badge, or, if allowed, students may want to put a badge of their choice on their *gi*. In either case, do not attach the badge directly to your *gi*; instead, sew Velcro to the suit and fix the other side to the back of the badge to allow for removal during washing and to enable it to come away easily if an opponent's foot or hand gets caught on it during sparring.

must know
Do ask your instructor if it is all right to put a badge on your *gi*, then clear it with him or her as to what designs or styles are permitted.

In spite of what the manufacturer might claim, until you have positively proved that your coloured karate belt is colourfast, it is not a good idea to wash it with your *gi*.

Belts

The colour of the karate belt signifies the wearer's rank or grading (*kyu* or *dan*, see page 180), and therefore as part of the *gi* it is held in great reverence. Karate belts are usually made of cotton, around 2.5 metres (8 feet) long and 4 cm (1¼ in) wide – your ideal karate belt length should be three times your waist measurement. Black belts are usually slightly wider than belts of other colours, featuring ten or twelve lines of lengthways stitching as opposed to six or eight for the lower ranks.

Belts are worn wrapped twice around the body, just above the hips and below the waist, over the *gi*'s jacket. Although there should be some play, the belt should not be loose enough to allow fingers or toes to get caught in it. The ends will be passed around the body and tied in front in a loose reef knot – there is much debate about whether or not the belt should cross at the back, so it is a good idea to ask the instructor if that club has any rules about this. The ends should hang down towards the floor and be the same length.

In very traditional karate schools, black belts will not be dyed all the way through, but will be white cotton covered in black. The idea is that since the black belt is seen not as the ultimate grade, but just another stage of the *karateka*'s journey, so, as time progresses, the black wears away to reveal the white underneath, reminding the wearer of how close they are to that first step.

Other kit

There isn't a great deal of other kit needed in karate until you start regular sparring sessions, and then what students may be required to buy will vary enormously from club to club. Unless you are doing full contact karate – and you shouldn't be – you should not receive blows to the body or head, but most clubs will require you to wear some degree of protection – indeed it may be a condition of their insurance.

Groin protectors

A 'box', as it is called on the cricket pitch, is the most likely piece of equipment you will be asked to wear, because it will protect you from an accidental blow to the groin, which can be particularly unpleasant, for women as well as for men.

Mouthguards

These are the type of gum shields used by boxers or rugby players.

Arm, shin and instep padding

Few traditional clubs will even permit this, let alone require it, since their belief is that padding which dulls the contact of blocks and defensive technique creates a false impression of what a solid block feels like, and thus inhibits student development in this area.

Head guards

Again, seldom used in traditional clubs since sparring students are expected to respect their opponents and therefore should be very careful about where head-high kicks and punches land. Many teachers believe head guards can discourage carefulness.

Sparring gloves

Once again, these are not very common for the same reasons that head guards are rarely used.

must know

When buying karate suits for children, as they are still growing it is not a good idea to buy to fit. But if the suit is much too long, then turn them up inside and make sure you sew the hems securely, as just rolling them up won't last the lesson and could prove dangerous.

Karate etiquette

Because karate is based on a culture of respect and understanding, it has a strong code of etiquette. However, many of the rules are there for the safety of the participants.

The *karateka*'s code

1 Be punctual.
2 Pay attention to your personal hygiene.
3 Concentrate and listen carefully to the instructor.
4 Be respectful to all others, regardless of their rank.
5 Do your best at all times.

Respect

The biggest part of karate etiquette is respect for what you are doing and how you are doing it. This was looked at in The *Dojo* on page 14. Since you should have respect for the place at which your karate is practised; and, from the moment you enter and bow, you should be in a *karateka* frame of mind – you are there to learn and your concentration must be 100 per cent. This leaves no room for fooling about, chatting or horseplay.

Personal hygiene is paramount, which means keeping yourself and your *gi* clean, your hair cut or tied up appropriately, and your fingernails and toenails short. Jewellery or watches are not allowed in the *dojo*, and if you are wearing a T-shirt under your *gi*, as many women do, it should be white and clean. You will also be expected to keep the *dojo* clean and tidy – stow your gear neatly along the back wall and, if requested, carry out any cleaning tasks cheerfully.

Politeness to your teacher and fellow students will be a given, and this will extend to bowing instead of shaking hands, and bowing to your partner at the beginning and end of any paired exercises. If you have questions, ask the teacher or a senior student during an appropriate time; do not disrupt other students' tuition by speaking out during a session.

Karatekas **will bow to each other before starting any exercise.**

Rank, indicated by the colour of the belt, is very important when studying karate, and the club's natural order will be demonstrated when students line up in front of the teacher to receive instruction: it will be from left to right in order of ranking, with lowest ranking on the right, and if there is more than one line the higher grades will be in front. When classes are divided for some exercises it will be by rank, since that denotes experience and expertise. Senior students (black or brown belts) may well give instruction to lower *kyus*, who will treat them with the same respect and attention as they would the teacher. A club's senior black student will take the class in the absence of the teacher.

must know
Karate is built around a culture of respect, and this translates into bowing to opponents, higher grades and the *dojo* itself. This shouldn't be confused with any form of servitude.

Injuries and how to prevent them

Most karate injuries could be avoided; so often it is just a matter of commonsense and taking proper care. Below are the most widespread injuries and advice on how to treat them if they occur.

Common problems

A recent American survey of sports in general showed that, on average, *karateka* were likely to suffer 1 injury per 48 hours of training/practice (rugby scored 1 per 50 hours), with women twice as likely to suffer injury than men.

The most common injuries were sprains (stretching or tearing joints' connective ligaments) and strains (stretching or tearing muscles or the tendons that attach muscle to bone) and these are usually a result of an inadequate warm-up procedure or over-enthusiastic stretching. These should be treated with RICE – rest, ice, compression, elevation – followed by gentle mobility exercises; do not apply warmth as it will increase any swelling.

Shoulder, elbow and lower back problems are common and are usually caused by overuse and the very nature of 'snapping' karate's kicks and punches. Once again, attention to warming up and stretching can go a long way to protecting these areas, but the correct pacing of your learning and training schedule is important here. Rushing into performing too many kicks and punches before joints, tendons and support muscles have built up to cope with this activity will have a painful effect. Training needs to be approached gradually to allow the body to adjust to the increased demands of karate. Once again,

RICE is the best treatment for such injuries, but if the pain is intense consult your doctor as you may need anti-inflammatory medication.

There will always be cuts and bruises, but care taken in free sparring and observation of *dojo* dress and personal grooming guidelines (no jewellery, finger- and toenails kept short) are the best way to minimize them.

Six simple ways to prevent injury

1 Choose a club where the instructor concentrates on form, technique and calm rather than sparring and competition.

2 Do not train if there is anything physically wrong with you – if in any doubt, consult your doctor .

3 Warm up properly.

4 Wear whatever protective gear your club advises.

5 Exercise support muscles, and not just the ones you can see; these include abductor and rotator cuff muscles that hold up the back and hips while kicking and punching (see pages 110 and 134).

6 Be careful and respectful of your opponent and those around you.

Children's karate classes

In children's classes there should be no sparring among beginners, junior belts or those under the age of seven, and when it does take place a good club should recommend the use of gloves and head guards. When very young children start learning karate care should be taken that they do not overtrain because their bodies are growing rapidly and they will tire easily. One session a week should be the most they do.

want to know more?
• For more information on warming up and cooling down see page 46.
• To improve your physical fitness in general see chapter 3, page 32–55.
• Details of first aid courses in your area, which should cover sports injuries, can be found at: www.redcrossfirstaid training.co.uk
• For inspiration watch the film *Crouching Tiger, Hidden Dragon*.

3 Fitness and flexibility

Most people's idea of karate is the spectacular, gravity-defying kicks and darting, speedy punches, which will be a big part of your training's end product. However, the ability to undertake such fabulous feats is dependent on two basic tenets of karate training: fitness and flexibility. The first is mental as well as physical, and will give you the stamina and the speed of body and thought to spar and perform *kata* at the highest levels; while the latter will allow you to achieve movement and balance that could probably only be attempted by a ballerina!

Fit for karate

Although learning and practising karate is, in itself, a great way of getting or keeping fit, beginners will need to achieve a certain level of fitness in order to get the most out of their training. And students will also need to sharpen up their mental prowess.

Body and mind

Karate has always been its own best trainer. This is because, traditionally, it is the people's style, and because it first became widespread as an underground method of defence used by anti-government rebels. Thus it developed as a discipline able to be practised by anybody anywhere, regardless of their circumstances or environment, and learning it had to be done secretly, out of sight of the authorities. Which means that, although there are specific karate training and fitness aids used in many *dojos*, it is possible to attain a high level without using any accessories.

However, the benefits of using the repeated performance of the moves of your chosen style as your route to fitness are much more than just convenience. The drills will build only those muscles that you need for the best performances, and thus your body will not be weighed down – literally – with unnecessary muscle bulk; they will also go a long way to your attaining the muscle memory needed to act instinctively rather than consciously, and they will increase your flexibility (see page 50). Perhaps most importantly, however, this level of familiarity will promote a much better understanding of your style, what the moves are actually about and how

Practising karate moves such as this is an ideal way to keep fit.

they work. This last point is a vital part of the fitness of the mind that you will need to get to grips with, whatever style of karate you choose.

Mental outlook

Karate requires a great deal of focus, more so than many other sports, largely because it is potentially so dangerous. A *karateka* cannot afford to zone out or mentally drop off in the *dojo*, because it is so easy to injure yourself. If you are not doing your moves properly, or, when sparring, there is a real danger of hurting your opponent if you are not paying attention to your strikes.

Don't assume that, while you are training, you can plan what you are going to do at the weekend. Even during breaks in class, try not to hold conversations about outside matters – concentrate on karate.

Your outlook to mental effort should be the same as your outlook to physical training – you always have to try that little bit harder – since without the required mind power you won't get the best out of what you are doing. Karate is almost a science in its precision of internal and external effort, and enormous amounts of concentration will be required to ensure that punches, kicks and blocks are delivered using *all* the necessary muscles and movements. It will be the only way to properly harness your potential power.

As we shall see in the following pages, beyond simply practising karate, there are sets of basic exercises performed in the *dojo*. Each is simple and will involve no special equipment, allowing the *karateka* to keep themselves in top shape whatever situation they are in.

Learning karate will sharpen your concentration.

Physical fitness

In keeping with the notion of karate itself as being the most effective exercise, many clubs will use the slow movement method as a means of building up strength, whereby perfect punches and kicks are performed in slow motion – it's much harder than it might seem.

must know

Sit-ups should be performed with legs bent at the knees, so that the internal abdominals are relaxed and can be worked for increased flexibility.

Exercise

Holding stances for extended periods, or perhaps exaggerated in depth or length, are also widely used training exercises. In general, fitness exercises used at most karate clubs will be callisthenic, simple and designed to promote general toning, overall fitness and specific muscle development.

Sit-ups and press-ups are favourites, as they will work on the muscles that form the basis of punches and kicks. Sit-ups develop the stomach muscles, which are absolutely vital to good karate, as they provide protection if you take a blow to the midriff; they are what raise the upper part of the leg for kicking and will power the trunk-twisting that is used in several blocks.

Press-ups should be performed in a very specific manner. The hands should be no more than a shoulder width apart so that the arms remain close to the body and the movement will work the triceps instead of the pectorals. Also, it is usual to perform press-ups either on fingertips or on fists clenched karate-style, as this strengthens the hands and wrists and means you'll put more effort in general into the exercise. Ten or 20 clenched-fist press-ups are the usual forfeit for such infringements as being

Press-ups on palms, fists or fingertips are a staple karate training exercise.

late, talking, having a dirty *gi* or finishing last in a run or a contest.

Other exercises becoming popular are known as plyometrics, actions that build the sudden bursts of power used in karate. These work on a combination of speed and strength, to build power by repeating rapid muscle contractions. Beginners would not be expected to do these. The type of exercises common in *dojos* will be press-ups that see both the hands and feet leave the floor, perhaps with a hand clap before landing; vertical standing jumps; drop jumps (sometimes called burpees), when in between each vertical jump *karateka* will drop into a crouch and, with hands on the floor, shoot both feet out into a press-up position before returning to the crouch and the jump; and bunny-hops up and down the hall.

Weight training

Although it's far from unusual for *karateka* to work out with weights, it is not something most teachers will encourage, for several reasons. Karate is not about lifting anything or physical resistance; therefore, increasing your sheer strength will not lead to much improvement. Weight training can result in a bulking up of the muscles, which can slow movement and decrease suppleness; additionally, lifting weights is purely physical and can have no spiritual aspect, unlike so many karate exercises.

On the purely practical level, if you *are* going to pump iron alongside your karate training: a) use small weights and perform large numbers of fast repetitions (at least 20), increasing the reps and not the load as you get stronger; and b) tell your teacher you are doing it and seek his or her advice.

must know

Older *karatekas* should start with very gentle exercise and build up to the point at which the younger club members will start.

Something extra in the locker

There are also a couple of extra ideas you can bring to your fitness programme as you progress, each of which will benefit a different aspect of your karate training. If you will be doing a great deal of sparring, attain extra fitness by carrying out an intense aerobic exercise – skipping or stair-stepping – for the length of time of a round (usually two minutes), then resting for the time between rounds (one minute), and repeating twice more. This will prepare you for the timings of the concerted action of a bout. To improve your fitness for the lengthy *katas* required for the higher grades, stamina should be built up by prolonged medium-intensity exercise such as running, cycling or swimming – skating is particularly good as it helps with graceful movement and balance.

Roller blading and roller or ice skating will greatly help your balance and co-ordination.

Mental strength

In karate, fitness of the mind is as important as fitness of the body. While it will be technically possible to sleepwalk your way through the motions of training – and if your teacher lets you get away with it you deserve each other – you will never get the best out of it unless you are as mentally sharp as you can be.

must know

You cannot train for, or practise, karate while you are doing something else – for instance, watching television or plugged into your iPod – because your mind and body need to be working together; if not in perfect harmony, then definitely in unison.

Focus

The concentration required for karate operates on two levels. Firstly, there is the external concentration on what you are being told by your *sensei* and what is going on around you – i.e. your fellow students in the *dojo*. This comes from the culture of respect within the *dojo* (see page 14): everything your *sensei* tells you is for a reason, and you need to be aware of the people around you or partners you are sparring with. It is this consideration of what others around you are doing, or where they are, that goes a long way to preventing accidents within the class.

The second level of concentration is internal, focusing your strength and balance and movement into the action you are performing at the precise moment you are performing it. This isn't just a matter of concentrating and remembering how to execute a particular move, although that will be very necessary for beginners, but the degree of mind power needed to deliver awesome power and efficiency when sparring or performing *kata*.

Since few karate moves involve using merely one muscle or muscle group, to be effective you need to concentrate on getting everything working together and arriving at the right place at the exact time, with a concentration of force pushed up from within you. This state involves utter focus on what you are doing, which is something many instructors refer to as 'connection', and when it is achieved the mental and physical effort you have exerted will combine to become far greater than the sum of their parts – in other words, much more than just a straightforward punch or kick.

In both cases, your focus should remain intact throughout each lesson and your powers of concentration will increase as you progress as a student. This is because simply by concentrating on concentrating you will do it better and better – think of your brain as a muscle that can be developed by working out! Your improved levels of concentration will be something that will stay with you outside the *dojo* and you will find you will be able to concentrate on everyday tasks with a far greater degree of focus.

did you know?
Meditation is an important part of martial arts. In the early days practitioners believed they had to fully understand what they were doing in order to get the most out of every aspect. Today, many karate lessons still involve meditation.

Clear your mind of day-to-day business before you start training.

The karate diet

Good nutrition is vital to anybody wishing to learn karate; therefore, ensuring you maintain a healthy diet will be as important as laundering your *gi* between classes.

Your eating habits

When you start karate training, the chances are that you will be doing more exercise than your body is used to, and to be able to get the maximum benefit from it you will need to adapt what you eat. There are two stages to achieving the sort of healthy eating necessary for karate: the first involves removing the harmful foods and replacing them with good ones, while the second stage is concerned with the extra nutrition you should be taking on board.

Dump the junk

As soon as you begin practising karate, you should cut out processed or junk food, packaged snacks and large amounts of sugar. These are known as empty calories, because they deliver such relatively tiny amounts of energy and nutrients for their high calorific value. And because they offer so little, they satisfy the body for a very short space of time before you feel hungry again.

Although something sweet such as chocolate or a power bar will give you the instant energy rush you need right after a training session, processed or high sugar foods have no business as a large part of your diet. Because you will be expending more calories, you would end up eating far too much junk food, which would result in fatigue or weight gain or both.

Replace the processed food in your kitchen with fresh ingredients – they will contain many more nutrients. As for snacks, go for fresh raw vegetables such as carrots, celery, broccoli or strips of peppers; fresh fruit, or dried fruit such as raisins, sultanas or apricots. Drink water or fresh fruit or vegetable juice instead of fizzy drinks or squash.

Eating for training

Because you will be exercising often and regularly, you will need to increase your intake of three major nutrients: protein, carbohydrate, and omega-3 fatty acids. Between them, they will help you get stronger, have more energy to train and ease stiffness and soreness in the joints.

Protein is nature's builder, and you will need to take in more of it to build the muscle that regular karate training will start to develop. Protein-rich foods include red meat, chicken, fish, milk and dairy products, beans, nuts and tofu. Per day you should be consuming 1 gram of protein for every kilogram you weigh; this should increase to about 1.5 grams when you are starting out as a *karateka* as your body will be changing, and then to around 1.3 grams as you settle down into a training routine.

Carbohydrates are your main source of energy, so any karate-training regime will mean you are expending extra energy and will need to compensate for this by taking extra calories on board. There are two sorts of carbs: simple and complex. The former is sugar, which is quickly absorbed into the bloodstream and will speedily deliver a short-term boost – a sugar rush. Fruit and dairy contain simple carbohydrates. Complex carbohydrates are much slower acting, and as a longer-lasting energy source will bring greater benefit during and after training. These are also called starches and can be found in pasta, potatoes, grain products and rice.

Omega-3 fatty acids are oils that are vital to keep the body lubricated, yet have to be taken in from outside as the body cannot produce them itself. Cold-water fish such as salmon, mackerel, herring, anchovies and sardines (also known as oily fish) are rich in these oils and will help relieve any discomfort from ligament or tendon wear and tear that results from karate training.

Swap processed food for fresh vegetables.

Carrots are an ideal snack, keep them in the fridge.

Eating salads will boost your water intake.

Eat nuts instead of crisps or sweets.

Eggs are a major source of protein.

Oily fish will keep your joints from creaking.

Few people drink enough water during the course of the day.

Drink more water

Water consumption is vital to your well being. Taking on enough water helps move nutrients, vitamins and minerals into the system quicker. It also prevents fatigue, since when the body's water levels are low water is drawn from the bloodstream, thickening the blood and needing more energy to keep it moving around the system. Additionally, since water can account for up to 75 per cent of your body weight, and the average adult loses up to 1.5 litres (2½ pints) per day through sweat, urinating and breathing (vapour), it needs constant replenishing. Yet few people drink enough water: men should drink at least 3 litres (5 pints) per day, and women 2 litres (3½ pints), and this consumption should increase if the weather is warmer.

When you are karate training, the need to keep yourself hydrated is even more acute, as you will sweat out a great deal during a session – on a karate-training day intake should be increased by about 30 per cent. Therefore, you should drink plenty of water before and after a class, and, if the *sensei* allows it, during the session. It is very important to remember to wait until given permission to drink in the *dojo* (see *Dojo* Etiquette, page 15), but most good teachers will be aware of their students' needs.

must know

It is very common to think you are hungry when you are, in fact, thirsty, and this leads to one of the most prevalent causes of overeating. Indeed, by the time you are aware of feeling thirsty, you are already dehydrated.

Warming up and cooling down

To stay injury-free, warming up properly is a vital part of any karate session, as the strains put on joints, muscles and ligaments are unique and far more acute than other forms of exercise. Equally important is cooling down.

Warming up

The theory behind warming up (for any sport, not just karate) is to gently ease the body through the transition from resting to intensely active and so prepare it for the increased stresses and strains in a way in which it can safely cope. To go from a standing start to vigorous punching or high kicking would put such sharp tension on muscles and tendons that are still contracted or tight that sprains, strains, tears or internal bruising would be the most likely result. As well as the injury potential, a cold body simply will not perform as efficiently as one that has been properly warmed up because it will not move as freely.

Warming up exercises are divided into four categories, with each fulfilling a different function as they combine to raise the heart rate, relax muscles, loosen joints and jog the memory.

Pulse warmers

These aerobic exercises will increase the heart rate from the usual resting rate of around 70 beats per minute (bpm) to a more action-friendly 150 bpm. Why this is important is because gradually raising the heart rate will avoid the potential strain of a bpm spike that would occur if you went straight into action. The increased heart rate allows blood to flow quicker, which moves more blood to the muscles, thus loosening them up, and also provides extra oxygen to the muscles being exerted, thus preventing any early breathlessness. Ideal pulse warmers for the *dojo* are running, running on the spot, or jumping jacks.

Stretching

Because karate kicks involve raising the legs to what are, essentially, unnatural levels, muscle stretching is an integral part of learning and practising and therefore stretching will be dealt with in a section of its own (see page 50). However, some initial stretching, a relatively gentle easing out of the muscles as opposed to the progressive loosening of karate's intense stretching, should be part of the warm-up routine. This is vital because it further loosens the fibres of the muscles, allowing the increased blood flow to penetrate easier; also, by gradually increasing muscle elasticity it avoids the chance of a tear or a sprain when proper activity begins. And finally, a loosened muscle is far less likely to bruise than a tight one, as the relaxed fibres will absorb a much greater impact. Legs, back, shoulders, trunk and arms should be stretched out during warming up.

A good stretching session will release endorphins and make you feel good all over.

Ballistics

Often referred to as 'mobility exercises', these loosen the joints by relaxing their connective tissue and so increasing the flow of synovial fluid, your joints' natural lubricant. This will prevent internal bruising or straining of joints and allow for more efficient

Running on the spot or jumping jacks will get the blood flowing.

mobility. Short, rapid jumping is best for the ankles and knees; the waist and hips should be rotated; likewise, shoulders and neck; while elbows and wrists need to be shaken out.

Skills rehearsal

This is your mental warm-up, the part that reactivates muscle memory to facilitate your actions becoming instinctive rather than conscious. Although a large part of your karate lesson's practice, before sparring or *kata*, will be exactly this – skills rehearsal – it's still important to incorporate it into your warm-up routine as a way of making sure everything is working. You can always go back to another stretch or ballistic exercise. It's why you see footballers or cricketers taking air shots before they start to play.

Warming down

Warming down correctly is probably more neglected than warming up, but it is equally important, and will help you to avoid the aches and pains that often follow exercise.

As the name might suggest, the purpose of warming down is the opposite of warming up – under your control, it gradually returns the body to normal after a period of intense activity. While warming down gently reduces your heart rate, it fulfils another major function by dispersing the lactic acid from your muscles. During intense physical activity, your muscles break down the glucose supplied by the blood to use as fuel, and a by-product of this is lactic acid. During activity it is pumped away from the muscles and disposed of within the body, but when you stop exercising it will still be produced for a few minutes but not dispersed, and it is this excess that, if it is allowed to remain in your muscles, will cause the ensuing stiffness and soreness. Gradually slowing exercise, stretching and, ideally, a massage will prevent any lactic acid remaining.

The four steps to warming down

1 Reduce heart rate with gradually decreasing aerobic activity.

2 Disperse excess lactic acid with gradually reducing mobility exercises.

3 Stretch out and massage muscles as they return to normal density.

4 Take a hot shower to further relax your naturally tightening muscles.

Stretching

Since being able to kick beyond the usual range of mobility is a large part of what makes karate so dynamic, stretching your sinews to achieve such movement is fundamental.

Flexibility

Loose, stretched muscles and tendons are the key to the mobility required to perform even the most basic karate moves, and as you progress up through the levels, the more flexible you are the greater advantage you will have over an opponent. Once you've warmed up, stretching will be an important part of your preparation for class – it's not unusual to have 15 minutes devoted to stretching. Different stretches will be carried out either by yourself or with a partner of approximately the same height.

Unless the stretch is a twisting or arching movement, *keep your back straight while stretching*. Although it will sometimes be easier to reach greater limits of leg lift by bending your back, it will not give you any long-term benefit, since a bent back means your pelvis isn't rotating fully. One of the main purposes of leg stretching is to ease the connection of leg muscles to the pelvis, and this can only be properly achieved if the pelvis is allowed to rotate – thus a flat back is the basis of an effective leg stretch.

The correct breathing during stretching is very important, as it will relax your diaphragm and will have a calming effect on your state of mind as you begin your lesson. Breathe in deeply through your nose as you start the stretch, exhaling slowly through your mouth as you hold the position.

Basic stretches

Seated toe touch (hamstrings/calves)
1 Sit on floor with legs straight out to the front and grab ankles or feet.

2 Keeping back as straight as possible, pull face down to knees.

must know

Stretch every day, whether you are training or not, as frequent, gradual stretching is much more likely to produce lengthened, supple muscles than occasional intense bouts.

Toe touch (back and hamstrings)
1 Stand with feet slightly apart, and arms reaching straight up over your head.

2 Bend from the waist – keeping the back straight – as far down as you can. Grab your ankles (or shins) to pull yourself further down and hold.

3 Aim to put your face on your knees or your palms on the floor.

Final position (front view, left leg forwards)

Final position (side view, right leg forwards)

Lunge stretch (hips)

1 Stand with feet 1–1.2 metres (3–4 feet) apart, turn into front stance position (front leg bent at right angle at knee, back leg straight with heel off floor), hands on hips.

2 Keeping body straight, push hips downwards and hold.

3 Turn through 180 degrees to reverse stance, push down and hold.

Crouch stretch (hips and hamstrings)

1 Stand with feet 1–1.2 metres (3–4 feet) apart, turn to left, bend right knee forwards and raise ball of left foot, keeping heel on floor.

2 With arms outstretched and hands together (palms facing outwards), lower body into stretch by bending right leg and keeping left leg straight.

3 Hold at lowest point – eventually you will be virtually sitting on the floor with left foot pointing upwards.

4 Rise into upright position, turn and repeat with right leg straight.

Final position (arms outstretched in front of you)

Alternate final position (with arms pointing to the left)

must know

Regular stretching will have benefits beyond your karate class, as relaxed muscles reduce physical and mental stress on the body, making sleep easier and reducing so many of life's general aches and pains.

Front stretch (groin and hips)

1 Sit on floor with legs straight and spread as wide as possible; toes should be pointing straight up.

2 Keeping back straight, bend forwards from waist with hands reaching out on floor in front of you.

3 Rotate your hips forwards, touch your chin on the floor and hold.

● Experienced *karateka* will do this stretch in pairs, with the partner either standing behind and pushing down on the stretchee's back, or sitting opposite them with feet placed inside the stretchee's knees and pulling.

Side front stretch (hamstrings and hips)

1 Sit on floor with legs straight and spread as wide as possible; toes should be pointing straight up.

2 Keeping legs and back straight, turn to right, grab right ankle or foot with both hands.

3 Pull face down to right knee and hold.

4 Straighten up, turn and repeat to left knee.

Hamstring stretch

1 Sit on floor with left leg extended (toes pointing straight up) and right leg bent, with sole of foot pulled in as close to groin as possible.

2 Grab ankle or foot of extended leg, pull chest to knee and hold.

3 Straighten up and repeat move with right leg extended.

Progressing to kick stance

As you progress in your chosen style, time will be taken in each class to stretch into kicks. This takes place after the individual stretches and is executed with a partner. Each person will pair up with somebody of approximately the same height and weight and stand just short of a kick's length in front of each other. One partner executes a kick in slow motion and the other catches the kicking foot. The foot is then lifted to the highest point possible with the kicker still maintaining his or her balance. The kicker is trying to achieve a position in which the foot finishes higher than it would naturally when kicking and there should be some tension felt in the kicking leg. The foot lifter should be very careful to raise the foot gradually so as not to cause any injury. This procedure should be carried out once per session with each leg for every kick.

want to know more?

• To learn more about stretching read:
Ultimate Flexibility: A Complete Guide to Stretching for Martial Arts by S. H. Kim (Turtle Press, US).

• Studying and practising yoga techniques will greatly help you to achieve maximum flexibility.

• The British Wheel of Yoga is a nationwide network of yoga teachers and courses and will help you find one in your area. It can be contacted at: www.bwy.org.uk

4 Balance and movement

At the basis of all karate styles is balance. To stay balanced while you perform movements is the most important thing you'll learn, and everything else will progress from there. Good balance begins with strong stances, and this section deals with standing firm and being ready to move forcefully in any direction.

Balance and solid stances

A *karateka*'s stance is like the foundations of a building: get it right and what's built on top of it will have strength and durability; get it wrong, however, and don't expect it to be upright for too long!

must know

Standing still in exaggerated karate stances - that is, in a slightly lower than standard position - will help you to develop the muscles used to keep those stances strong.

Stances

Without a strong stance it is impossible to deliver all of your potential power in a punch or a kick or a block; and in sparring situations, starting or finishing a move off balance will leave you very vulnerable to your opponent's counterattacks. For these reasons, any beginner should be very aware that all techniques – punches and blocks, as well as kicks – draw their power from the legs. A correctly executed karate move pushes up from the floor with the soles of the feet, and the power can be felt surging through the standing leg or legs through the torso and into the active arm or leg. However, power can only be harnessed in this way if the legs have solidly planted feet to push against.

A flimsy stance will result in the only power put into the move being generated by the arm or leg concerned. This will not only mean the move will be weaker than it should be, but also, any temptation to compensate by over-exertion from an unanchored stance could lead to loss of balance or even joint damage.

For this reason, the four basic karate stances – front, back, riding and side – are all firmly planted and create the firmest possible platform from which to launch and maintain a move.

Getting your stance right can be psychologically important, too. A weak stance will be seen by others – your instructor or your opponent – as a sign of weakness of approach and will either be exploited on the sparring mat or marked against you when you are being considered for gradings. A strong, powerful-looking stance, however, will have the opposite effect. Also, standing firm and strong will give you a mental boost that will translate into your entire training schedule, since it will help you to focus on what you are doing and be far more aware of your body and its potential.

Standing correctly may be a bit uncomfortable in the beginning, but by simply doing so you will be strengthening your leg muscles, and ultimately making your stances easier and stronger.

Balance

Superior balance will always be the difference between a good *karateka* and a great one. From a well-balanced stance you should be able to move in any direction or execute any attacking or defensive move to the best of your abilities. If your stance gives the move its power, the balance allows it to happen in exactly the way you intended. Also, as well as leaving you best prepared for whatever move you plan to make next, good balance throughout a move will leave you far less vulnerable to counterattack from your opponent. And finally, that feeling of being off balance as you execute a move can affect everything else: it will sap your confidence as you continue, and provide so much to worry about that you will end up making other mistakes.

Good balance begins with stability, and the four

must know
Pair up with a *karateka* of approximately the same height and weight and take it in turns to try to push each other out of stances. It will help you to strengthen them.

basic stances all keep the entire sole of the foot planted firmly on the ground with the ankle flexing to help steadiness. The knees will always be slightly flexed (except for the front stance's rear leg), which allows for mobility and lowers the hips. This lowering of the hips is crucial, as it allows the stance to be nearer the ground, lowering the centre of gravity and thus making it more stable, but it is done with the body kept bolt upright. Such a posture is vital to maintain good balance, as it allows you to move in any direction without having to waste time or energy compensating for leaning over in another direction, and means all moves will be more controlled, since they will all start from the same place.

Ready stance (*Yoi-dachi*)

Often called the 'parallel stance', it is the first stance, the one you take when you are lined up in front of your instructor, about to begin a class or an exercise sequence. It is the stance you will assume before going into any of the other stances in this section, because from it you should be 'ready' for anything, and thus will be equally balanced to take up any other stance.

Position of feet

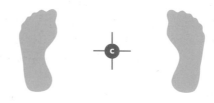

c = centre of gravity

The ready stance is upright and alert.

In the ready stance, you will be standing with your feet a shoulder width apart, knees slightly bent, dropping the hips a little; the back will be perfectly straight and the shoulders held square. Hands will be lightly closed into loose fists held a few inches away from the body, and eyes will be looking forwards, alert and ready.

To move into it from a relaxed position – when your instructor yells '*Yoi*' – you should slide your right foot out to gain the stance, while squaring your shoulders and closing your hands.

Front stance (*Zenkutsu-dachi*)

The most used stance in karate, this one has 60 per cent of the weight on the front foot, thus keeping the back foot light for kicking. The stance is naturally aggressive with an inherent forward thrust, making it the ideal position from which to throw a powerful punch or perform a strong block.

From the ready stance, slide the left foot forwards, bending the left knee but keeping the right leg straight, until the feet are approximately twice as far apart from front to back as they are from side to side – the stance should be two shoulder widths by one shoulder width. The body remains upright, with the hips dropped, and the shoulders turned slightly to the side. The left foot points directly forwards, the right foot will be pointing forwards at an angle – the more flexible your ankles become, the more that (right) foot will face to the front.

must know

Executed correctly, the front stance is one of the strongest karate stances there is. An instructor will often try to push a student off balance out of their front stance, and if the student is doing it well the instructor will not be able to.

Position of feet

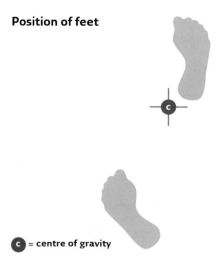

c = centre of gravity

- Shoulders and hips turned slightly to the side.
- Front foot facing forwards.
- Back foot at 45 degrees.
- Feet at shoulder width apart.
- With arm straight, the leading fist faces downwards over the leading knee.
- Opposite fist is chambered.

Final position
(front view)

Final position
(side view)

- Body upright.
- Front leg bent at the knee.
- Rear leg straight.

must know

Although essentially
a defensive stance,
because so much of
your weight is on your
back foot it is an ideal
position from which
to launch swift and
surprising front foot
strikes such as snap
kicks, or leading
hand jabs.

Back stance (*Kokutsu-dachi*)

This is a classic defensive or retreating stance,
distributing the weight at a ratio of approximately
70/30 between the back and front foot, respectively.
Because of this balance, your centre of gravity will
be pitched much further back and the natural
movement will be backwards.

From the ready stance, slide the right foot back,
bringing it in line with the front foot, turning the
right foot and knee outwards to a 90-degree angle
with the left and bending both knees. Stop when a
distance of approximately two shoulder widths has
been reached. Your weight should be over the back
leg, with the front foot light on the ground. The feet
are in line and the body is turned side-on – you look
over one shoulder – thus presenting your opponent
with as narrow a target as possible.

Position of feet

c = centre of gravity

- Feet in a line.
- Back knee and back foot at 90-degree angle.
- Body side on to present smallest target.
- With leading arm slightly bent, the palm is facing outwards to protect the face.
- Opposite fist is chambered.

Final position
(front view)

Final position
(side view)

- Feet two shoulder widths apart.
- Body upright.
- Back leg bent at a slightly greater angle than the front.
- Weight ranged to rear of stance.
- Right hand is chambered ready to strike.

Riding stance (*Kiba-dachi*)

Often called the horse stance or straddle stance, this gains its name because, if done correctly, it looks like you are sitting on a horse. This strong, rooted stance is the most basic of all karate stances and is used frequently in training for static punching and blocking drills. It is also useful as an exercise in itself, as time spent in the riding stance will strengthen hips, legs and ankles.

From the ready stance, slide the right foot to the right until your feet are approximately two shoulder widths apart. With hips and shoulders square-on to the front and keeping the back dead straight, lower the hips by bending the knees, and settle into a seated position. Feet should be parallel and facing forwards and your shins should be as close to right angles with the floor as you can keep them. Your weight should be distributed equally on your legs.

Position of feet

c = centre of gravity

- Shoulders and hips square-on to the front.
- Feet parallel, two shoulder widths apart.
- Knees facing forwards.

- Back straight.
- Feet facing forwards.
- Shins as upright as possible.
- Hips lowered into seated position.

must know

As an exercise, assume a riding stance and, while keeping your back straight, lower the stance by dropping your hips a few inches straight down. Hold this position for a few seconds and return to a normal riding stance, then repeat. As you get stronger, you will be able to go down lower and hold the position longer.

Cat stance (*Neko-ashi-dachi*)

Because the front foot has virtually no weight on it, and that leg is cocked ready for action, this is an ideal stance for front foot attacks. It is also a good protective stance as the body is placed further back and the groin presents a difficult target.

From the ready stance, shift your weight entirely on to your right foot, bending the knee. As you do so, push your left leg forward, turning the body to present a side-on target, raising the left hand to shoulder height – either as a clenched fist or knifehand (see page 165) – and chambering (see glossary page 184–5) the right fist. This is a very narrow stance and the feet are little more than a shoulder width apart. Settle 90 per cent of your weight on the back leg, and raise the heel of the front foot so it is resting on the ball of the foot and remains very mobile. Your centre of gravity should be very close to your back foot.

must know

During sparring, this stance is not held for too long; fighters will usually move into it quickly, kick and move out of it.

Position of feet

c = centre of gravity

- Shoulders and hips turned side-on.
- Front hand should be raised to shoulder height.

Final position
(front view)

Final position
(side view)

- Heel of front foot raised.
- Weight 90 per cent on back foot.
- Hips lowered.
- Right hand is chambered ready to strike.

Side stance (*Sesan-dachi*)

This is often called the Side-facing riding stance, simply because that's pretty much what it is. It differs from the riding stance inasmuch as your head will be turned to the direction in which you are about to move and you will be looking over that shoulder. It is a more mobile and 'prepared' stance than the riding stance, ideal for delivering side-kicks or knife-hand strikes, since you will be poised to move sideways without turning or adjusting any part of your body.

From the ready stance, turn your head to the right to look over your right shoulder. As with the riding stance, slide the right foot to the right until your feet are approximately two shoulder widths apart. With hips and shoulders facing the front and the back straight, lower the hips by bending the knees, and settle into a seated position. Feet should be parallel and facing forwards and your shins should be as close to right angles with the floor as you can keep them. Your weight should be distributed equally on your legs. (In some schools, the leading foot may be turned outwards at a 45-degree angle.)

must know

The side stance is a very useful sparring stance, as it presents a narrow target to your opponent, is mobile either backwards or forwards, and perfect for attacking with a fast side kick.

The leading hand can be held in knife-hand or clenched-fist style.

Position of feet

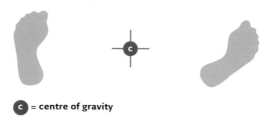

c = centre of gravity

- Shoulders and hips side-on.
- Head turned to the side.
- Feet and knees slightly angled, two shoulder widths apart.
- Left arm is slightly bent with upright knife hand.

Final position
(front view with
leading knife hand)

Final position
(side view with
leading clenched fist)

- Back straight.
- Feet slightly angled.
- Shins as upright as possible.
- Hips lowered into seated position.
- Right hand is chambered.

Fighting stance (*Kamae-dachi*)

This is a very relaxed, natural-feeling stance that will allow movement in any direction, and form the basis from where to carry out any move – attacking or defensive – swiftly and powerfully. It's a shorter, more upright stance than the ones we've just covered, and the feet will not be as firmly planted as in previous stances, to facilitate speed of movement over solid standing. This should not, however, compromise your balance before, during or after a movement, as it's during sparring that the value of good balance will become apparent.

From the ready stance, turn side-on to the right to face your opponent (to the left if you are left-handed). Slide your right foot forwards slightly to put your feet a little over a shoulder width apart; your right foot will face forwards, your left foot out at 90 degrees for better stability. Knees should be slightly bent and your weight distributed equally on your legs to facilitate swift movement in either direction. Hands should be loosely balled fists, with the right arm held up about 30 cm (12 in) in front of you, level with your face, and the left arm bent at the elbow to tuck the fist in close to your body just above your belt.

Position of feet

c = centre of gravity

must know

There are no real hard and fast rules for a fighting stance, merely guidelines for the beginner, because as a *karateka* becomes more experienced on the sparring mat so his stance will adapt to whatever he feels most comfortable with.

Attacking fight stance
- Weight evenly distributed.
- Hands poised to block or strike.
- Front foot is relaxed so cannot be swept.

Defensive fighting stance
(left handed)
- Weight slightly to the rear.
- Slightly bent knees.
- Feet at right angles for added stability.
- Left hand extended for defence.
- Right hand ready for reverse punch.

Footwork

Good footwork is the foundation of all karate movements, whether it is in *kata* or free sparring. So it's vital you spend time on what your feet are doing when they're not actually kicking.

must know

In the forwards and backward movement shown here, the feet move in and out as they slide forwards; this is to provide some protection for the groin and body during the step, although many karate schools will teach straight movement of the feet. It's not hard to adapt, and every other aspect of the steps is the same.

The slide

In free sparring, good footwork can make all the difference to how you perform. It will propel you into an attack or get you out of trouble when defending. Most of all, it will mean you can dictate the space between you and your opponent, and fight at a distance that is comfortable to you and not him – this can be very disconcerting and cause hesitancy in his attacks.

To be able to move efficiently, quickly and with power, you will slide along the floor rather than step, as this will save time, conserve energy and maintain your balance. Your body will remain upright and your head should stay at the same height.

Karate's basic steps are:

Stepping forwards – for this you should start in a front stance (see page 62)

1 If you are in a strong position and don't want to change your leading leg, this rapid forwards movement is ideal. It is also very good as a precursor to a front snap kick from your front foot, or a jab with your leading hand. Maintaining a continuous head height, slide the left foot up just behind the right foot (1a in diagram opposite), as soon as it makes solid contact with the ground push forwards with the right back into the front stance (1b). The hands shouldn't switch.

2 To switch your leading foot as you step forwards, slide the left foot up next to the right and, in one continuous

movement, forwards into a front stance with the left foot in front. Your hands will also have changed so the left hand is now in front (2), and will have done so by crossing over as a downward block (see page 88). Make sure that your hips change to the new stance, and do so with power.

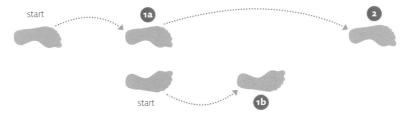

Stepping backwards – for this you should be in a back stance (see page 64)

1 To maintain your lead foot while stepping back, slide the right foot back until it is next to the left (1a), then slide the left foot back to settle into a back stance (1b) with your right foot and hand remaining in front.

2 To change your leading foot, bring the right foot back alongside the left and continue moving it back, to settle into a back stance with your left leg forwards (2). Your hands will shift lead by crossing over in an outward block, and don't forget to turn your hips.

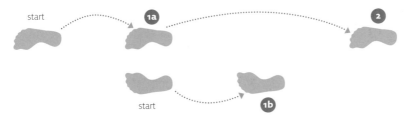

must know
The most common problems with stepping backwards are hesitancy and riding up in the stance, either of which can leave you unnecessarily vulnerable mid-step. Then there's the problem of the feet passing too close to each other and getting briefly tangled up. It's important to practise your footwork regularly.

Stepping sideways – for this you should be in a side stance (see page 70)

1 Maintaining an upright body and bent knees, while keeping your head at the same height, slide your left foot up to your right foot

2 Slide your right foot along to achieve another side stance of the same width.
NB Your hands will remain as they were, and you will keep looking over your right shoulder. Don't be tempted to cross your feet – beginners are likely to trip up.

start   start

Turning to face the rear – for this you should be in a front stance (see page 62)

1 Shift your weight on to your left foot (the rear foot), and turn to the right to look behind you over your right shoulder. Slide your right foot back to your left and as they become level swivel both feet 180 degrees (1).

2 Then slide your right foot forwards into a front stance, while your left foot completes the turn (2).
NB As you turn your arms will cross in front of you to finish with a downward block over your right knee.

must know
When you are turning, never forget to look behind you *before* you start the turn and *not* during.

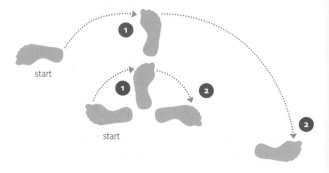

start

start

Ten basic rules of movement

1 Move on the balls of your feet.

2 Limit your movement to the direction in which you are travelling, so that a minimum of energy will be wasted – don't bob up and down.

3 Turn your hips explosively into each step to add power to whatever move you are doing.

4 When changing direction, turn your head before you turn your body. You will be able to see anything you might be turning into and avoid surprise attacks.

5 Be confident and decisive – hesitant movement will be taken advantage of by your opponent and your strike will lose power.

6 Time your steps so that the strike or block coincides with the step reaching its end, thus focusing all your power at the same time.

7 Step quickly – you are least able to defend while executing a step, and your opponent will know this.

8 Slide feet along the floor – raising them will slow the step down.

9 Come to an abrupt and complete stop; any wavering will mean you are off balance.

10 Use your footwork to maintain a distance between you and your opponent that you feel most comfortable with – don't let him dictate this space.

want to know more?
- **Take it to the next level. Practise combining movement with punches (see chapter 6, page 108), and movement with kicks (see chapter 7, page 132).**
- **It's a good idea to practise in a karate club environment, as many part-time *dojos* are situated in dance studios and have at least one mirrored wall for you to observe what you are doing and correct your mistakes.**
- **For advice on choosing the karate club that best suits your needs, see page 176.**

5 Defence

When martial arts were first developed in
China and Japan, the idea was for the people
to protect themselves against army brutality.
Even now, the fundamentals of so many
martial art forms have been developed with
self-defence in mind. For this reason, it follows
that good karate begins with good defence.
In this section we study defence as a series of
blocks that, if properly executed will protect
every vital part of the body. These blocks are
dynamic and can be as potentially disabling
as most attacking moves.

Defence is the best form of attack

Karate, at its essence, is a method of self-defence, and it follows that moves designed to protect your person form the basis of all karate teachings. Thus at any good karate school, before you learn to punch and kick, you will be taught *uke* technique, or how to block.

did you know?
Some martial arts styles have no blocks as part of the technique. In Tai Chi Chuan, for example, the philosophy is that blocking is a waste of energy, since it is merely using force to counter force; instead of direct blocks, it will utilize evasive and deflective techniques to make positive use of the opponent's energy.

Primary motive
Blocks are fundamental to karate, not only for protection, but also to leave you in the best possible position from which to launch a counterattack. This set of circumstances alone perfectly illustrates the philosophy behind so much martial arts teaching – defence is the primary motive, and only if an attack persists after it has been blocked should you launch a counterattack.

Different styles of martial arts will have different approaches as to how the emphasis is placed between attack and defence: Hapkido, for instance, is far more of a defensive art relying on evasive and controlling techniques, while the Korean Tae kwon do will focus on the block as the first step in a swift, powerful counterattack. There are even variations within the four main karate styles, with Goju-ryu and Wado-ryu being the most defensive-minded.

What all styles will have in common, however, is that they will all involve blocking manoeuvres, and the basic moves will all be very similar. This is because the aim of learning to block is always the same, and it goes further than merely protecting your head or torso. A *karateka* with an effective array of blocks in his technique will have the effect of creating an impenetrable sphere around his body, within which he will be able to formulate his attacks and avoid getting hurt. Also, most importantly, such an apparent force field will have a demoralizing effect on an opponent as they fail to land a meaningful blow.

The A-B-C of self-defence

Attack

All defensive techniques begin with an attack – somebody else's! Blocking is, philosophically, a non-aggressive action so, as a *karateka*, if there is no attack against you there is no reason for you to do anything.

Block

Protect yourself by stopping whatever strike is aimed at you. This alone should be your primary motive, to avoid getting hurt rather than inflicting any harm – of course, a well-delivered block can be an effective strike in itself.

Counterattack

If a strong, swiftly delivered block isn't enough to deter your attacker, then follow it through with an explosive and surprising counterattack. This should be as minimal and restrained as possible – ideally a single move, unless the situation calls for further force.

To be forearmed

In these basic karate blocks, the striking surface is the inside of the wrist or the forearms, and your technique will be much more effective, and safer for you, if you have well-developed forearm muscles. Remember, it is the muscle that is protecting the bone in your arm when you use it to block. If you do work out with weights, then reverse curls – with the palm facing down – will build up forearm muscle strength (see Chapter 3, Fitness and flexibility, page 32, for guidelines). Or, in a more traditional style, fingertip press-ups will work the same muscles and strengthen the wrists.

Maintaining the right distance is vital when blocking. Stay just over an arm's length away from your opponent.

Blocking technique

Uke (blocks) are the set of moves carried out to intercept an opponent's punch or kick and render it harmless by either stopping the blow dead or deflecting it away from your body. As self-defence is the primary concern, well-executed blocks will afford maximum protection, since nearly every blocking move will involve passing at least one of your limbs in a smooth sweeping action across the entire area of your body that is being attacked.

The blocking surface you will use to make contact is the inside of your forearm, just below the wrist. There, the covering of muscle is thicker yet the distance between the intended point of impact and your elbow will afford plenty of protection if the block hits slightly off target. Blocks should strike your opponent's attack with a rolling motion, as this will turn the inside of the forearm into the block and serve to lessen any impact as it rolls the strike away.

As in punching, speed and strength are at the heart of a good block: speed will allow you to arrive at the necessary blocking action before your opponent's strike gets there; while strength will ensure that the block holds up and does the job. Thus, the best way to approach blocking is in the same way as you would punching, and you should aim to snap the wrists in exactly the same way to focus the speed and strength you are deploying on the point of impact. To this end, it is important for the karate student not to draw too rigid a line between attack and defence, as a good block will fall into both areas. True, it prevents your opponent's attack, but it should also do some damage by breaking the flow of his movement or hurting whichever of his limbs it strikes.

must know

As you progress in your chosen form of karate, you will be taught to use your feet and legs to block, but these are advanced techniques and for the time being it is best to concentrate on using your arms.

Rather than viewing it as an action by itself, a block should be seen as the first step of the attack you will be launching. With the exception of the X block, all the blocks shown in this section are what are known as 'chamber actions', meaning that for every primary move you undertake (in this case the block itself) there will be an equal and opposite balancing movement. For instance, when the right arm is extended in a block, the left arm will come back close to the body with the fist poised just above the waist – the chamber position.

Such an action will greatly increase the power and accuracy of a block, and help the blocker stay on balance with his body in the correct position. It will also put you into the perfect position for delivering a swift punch as an effective counterattack. When practising blocks, once you have mastered the basic move, add a counterattack such as a front kick or a reverse punch.

The moves that will be covered in this chapter are the simplest and among karate's most effective. There are many more advanced and elaborate moves, but because of the straightforwardness of the following blocks, they are the most reliable in sparring or self-defence situations. Therefore, they tend to be favoured by even the most experienced *karateka*.

When we progress to the *kata* (see page 160) it will involve using the knife hand instead of the fist in some blocks. The movements of the block will be the same, the only significant differences will be that the hand is open with tensed, slightly curved fingers instead of a clenched fist. The knife hand is explained on p 165.

must know

When blocking in sparring or combat situations, remember to keep your fist clenched tight. This will reduce the risk of damage to your hand if the block doesn't land quite right, and will tense up your forearm for stronger contact if it does.

Practise, practise, practise

A slowly executed block will be even less effective than no block at all, since if it misses or arrives late not only will you receive the intended blow, but you will also be out of position to launch any counterattack. Thus blocks have to be carried out with great speed, which means that both as an action and a reaction they have to be second nature to you rather than a conscious decision. By the time you have thought about blocking before you actually block, you will already have been hit.

The only way to achieve this is by frequent and lengthy practice of the blocking actions, both by yourself and with a partner. Good karate clubs will always ensure that students train at defensive techniques as much as they do the showy stuff such as kicks and punches, and don't ever feel shy about getting some extra practice in, even if it's just 15 minutes a day in front of your bedroom mirror.

In a well-executed downwards block, the fist finishes outside the knee for maximum protection.

must know

Whatever stance you adopt when performing a block, it will not only need to be solid to add strength to the block itself, but also light enough to enable moving out of it at speed. This is because a block is far more likely to be followed by counterattack moves than a punch, which could well be the final act of such a sequence.

Blocking stances

All blocks shown will be practised from a riding stance, initially without stepping. This is because it is important to get the action of the block right from a static position, before having to worry about what your feet are doing.

However, another important factor for starting from a riding stance is that from it you can easily and quickly step in any direction. All the blocks on the following pages will be equally effective from whatever stance they are performed – front, back, side or riding – and when we get to the blocking drills (see page 98) the exercises will involve moving forwards and backwards while blocking into a front and back stance.

For an X block you need a particularly strong starting stance.

The left fist chambers back ready for a punch. **Keep it tucked in snugly against the body.**

Chamber action

Every karate block shown in this section (with the exception of the X block) is a chamber action (see above) which means that you will perform a movement of equal force opposite to the actual block. This will serve to focus the block's force into the intended area and make sure the blocker stays well balanced. Also, as the standard chamber position brings the non-blocking hand tightly back to a punching position it is ideal to launch a counterattack from this stance.

When you are learning blocking techniques, it is important to remember that as much attention should be paid to the 'chambering' as to the actual block itself.

Downwards block (*Gedan-uke*)

Probably the most widely used block in karate, the downwards block is used to protect the lower torso and groin against lower-aimed kicks and punches. Also, when it is used while stepping forwards it can intercept and cut off all front kicks before they get above waist height.

The direction of this block is downwards, and the movement sweeps across the body to finish just outside the line of the torso so that any punch or kick is deflected beyond an area where it could do any damage.

Performing the downwards block

From the riding stance with both fists clenched, bend your left elbow and raise your arm level with the top of your head, while moving your right arm up above your left shoulder with the palm facing towards your left ear (see above opposite). At this point, the raised left arm will protect your head.

Then start to bring your left arm backwards and at the same time, begin sweeping your right fist downwards. Your right wrist should rotate and your fist should finish just above your right knee, with the palm facing slightly away from you. As it does so, the left arm, which has been protecting the body while the block is being performed, is chambered back and poised to punch (see below opposite).

Remember to keep your body square-on and upright throughout the movement. Also finish the block as crisply as you would a punch with a defined snap. This will help you to stay in control of the movement and will stop you 'throwing' it out too far leaving you off balance and vulnerable to attack.

Start position

• Start with both fists clenched, bent left arm raised and right fist above left shoulder, palm turned in towards the ear.

• As the right fist comes down, performing the sweeping motion of the block, the left fist moves backwards.

• Finish the block with your left fist just above the knee and outside of the body line to ensure complete protection; the left arm should be close in to the side with the fist turned so the palm is facing upwards.

Final position

Rising block (*Age-uke*)

When deployed against an attack coming straight at your face – that is, an upper punch or a side kick – this is a particularly effective block, as it will get under your opponent's move. This will throw him off balance, as well as putting you in very close for a sharp counterattack.

The rising block holds the blocking arm bent at approximately 45 degrees and hinges it from the shoulder up from the top of the chest to just above the head, in a motion that travels in front of the entire throat and face. By finishing above the head, it is also very useful against an overhead strike.

Performing the rising block

From the riding stance with both fists clenched, bend your right arm and move it in front of you. Bend your left arm at the elbow to about 45 degrees and bring your fist to just below your right elbow joint, with the palm facing downwards (see above opposite).

As the right hand chambers backwards, the left hand raises upwards, still bent at a 45-degree angle. The left hand finishes just above the head to ensure that the entire area has been protected, while the right hand finishes just above the waist with the arm tucked in close to the side (see below opposite). Keep your body square-on and upright throughout the movement.

As with all blocks, you should finish with a crisp snap to ensure that you are completely in control of the movement. With the rising block though, it is particularly important that you don't watch the block land as this would move your eyeline in a such a way as to make you vulnerable to a low level attack.

must know

When practising blocking by yourself, make sure that you snap into the final position exactly as you would for a punch to ensure maximum strength in the movement. But do so without losing your balance so that you stay in control of the movement. You should hear your *gi* snap as you make the move.

Start position

• Start with both fists clenched, bend your right arm and move it in front of you, bend your left arm at a 45-degree angle, with fist under right elbow, palm facing downwards.

• Move your right arm backwards and roll your left arm upwards, keeping it bent at the same angle.
• The left arm finishes just above the head, while the right fist has chambered back to just above the waist.

Final position

Inside block (*Uchi-uke*)

Designed to protect the middle and upper parts of the body, the inside block uses an upright forearm sweeping diagonally across the torso, coming from inside to finish just outside the body line. It is most effective for deflecting straight strikes.

The blocking arm will be bent at the start of this move, and will come from under the extended arm to pivot across the body and finish with the forearm upright to protect as much of the torso as possible as it moves across.

Performing the inside block

From the riding stance with both fists clenched, move the left arm straight in front of you, and bring your right fist, palm down, under the upper part of your left arm. The right elbow should be bent at about 90 degrees and lower than the right fist (see above opposite).

As the left hand chambers backwards, the right forearm pivots at the elbow to move across the body and out to just outside the body for maximum protection. The elbow remains bent at the same angle and the forearm rolls round so that the block finishes with the right palm facing backwards. The left hand finishes just above the waist, while the body remains square-on and upright throughout the movement (see below opposite).

Finishing with a crisp snap is very important with this block, because if the movement is uncontrolled and travels too far past your body, it will leave your whole upper body square-on and open for counterattack. Also, for this reason, make sure that you go into your next move as quickly as you can.

good to know

Extending the opposite fist to your blocking arm, into the centre of your stance, will make sure your opponent keeps his distance while you are performing the block. It also assists with balance while you are moving rapidly.

Start position

• Start with both fists clenched, left arm extended in front of you and right arm bent at 90 degrees at elbow, with fist under upper part of left arm.

• Pull your left arm backwards and move your right fist forwards.
• The right fist finishes with the palm facing backwards and about level with the middle of the face, with the left hand tucked in just above the waist.

Final position

Outside block (*Soto-uke*)

This is a powerful block, which sweeps around from outside the body to cover the upper torso, throat and lower part of the face. It will involve a change of body position to swivel slightly into a side stance, which is very good for launching a side-kick counterattack.

The blocking arm will start from a position beyond the line of the body and therefore it has to be executed quickly and with strength and confidence, since, unlike the previous blocks, the body will be open at the start of the move. As the blocking arm moves in, the move is given added power by a twist off the trunk that will leave your body side-on to your opponent.

Performing the outside block

From the riding stance with both fists clenched, bend your left arm and move it across your chest towards your right shoulder for immediate protection. Bend your right arm at 90 degrees and move it in a backwards and upwards direction away from your body so that your fist is just behind your head, palm facing forwards (see above opposite).

As the left hand chambers back, the right arm, remaining bent at a 90-degree angle, is swivelled inwards from the shoulder along a line that keeps the fist just below eye level. When the right arm's inward rotation has gone as far as it can from the shoulder, you should continue the move by twisting your body from the waist so that the blocking arm travels past the torso. The final position will be with the left fist chambered by the waist, but the body will be turned slightly to the side (see below opposite).

must know

When executing the outside block, make sure your fist does not finish in front of your face as it could obscure your sight of your opponent for a vital split second or two. The final position of this block can be enhanced if the body is twisted even further to the side so that you end up looking over your right shoulder.

Start position

• Start with both fists clenched, left arm across the chest towards shoulder, right arm bent at 90 degrees, outside your body line, to the right, with fist just behind your head and level with your ear.

• As the left hand draws back, bring the right fist round on a horizontal line just below your eyes with the forearm as near to vertical as possible.
• In the final position your right fist should be just past your body line and still at eye level. The left fist will be back by your waist.

Final position

X block (*Juji-uke*)

This block is particularly good if you want to trap an opponent's hand or foot instead of merely stopping or deflecting his attack. It is a block of medium difficulty, but is worth practising at this point because it is so different to the others.

There are two types of X block: the rising and the downwards, which are both essentially the same movement except one is delivered to groin level and the other is overhead.

From the riding stance with both fists clenched, chamber each fist so they are at either side of your body just above the waist, with palms facing upwards. Shoot both arms out simultaneously to meet and cross in the centre of your body's axis either just below your groin or just above your head. Your arms will cross at the wrists, so the extended fists form the X, and the wrists are turned over as they meet, so that at impact the palms are facing down (lower X block) or forwards (rising X block). Keep body square-on and upright throughout the movement.

Start position
For both the downwards and rising X block (shown opposite), both fists should be chambered back to just above the waist, palms facing upwards.

Downwards X block

Shoot both fists out at the same time, towards your body's central axis. Arms will meet and cross at the wrists just below your groin, protecting you from any kick from directly below.

Rising X block

As for the downwards X block, shoot both fists out at the same time, towards your body's central axis. Arms will meet and cross at the wrists just above your head, protecting you from any strike from directly above.

Simple blocking drills

These are the very basic blocking drills, designed to familiarize yourself with the mechanics of each block, to get the feel of some sort of contact, and to help you build up your speed.

Blocks with a step

These drills are performed by yourself, so you can practise and perfect the techniques of blocking without having the distraction of making contact. It will serve to increase your confidence as well as your speed and actions. In the previous section the blocks are performed from a static stance, you will now take a step forward with each block – just as you would when sparring – but step back in between each to repeat the block using the other arm.

The photographs illustrate left arm blocks, but these drills should be performed with alternate arms.

Take up a ready stance, feet shoulder width apart, knees slightly flexed, arms slightly extended to the front and both fists clenched. As you perform each block, step forward into a strong front stance, positioning your body side-on so as to present as narrow a target as possible. With the exception of the X blocks, in each case the other fist chambers back ready for a reverse punch.

Begin by taking the step and making the block slowly, to ensure that you get the action absolutely right – make sure even the slow moves have plenty of power. Then speed up to step into the block quickly and powerfully; a *kiai* (a loud yell, see glossary, page 185) often helps at this point.

Downwards block

1 Start in ready stance, with fists clenched.

2 Step forward into front stance, raising left arm and turning body to the side.

3 Complete the block and step at the same time. Make sure the block finishes past the knee.

Rising block

1 Start in ready stance, with fists clenched.

2 As you step forward, bring your right fist up to just below eye level with your left arm crossed underneath it.

3 Chamber the right arm back, and roll your left arm upwards, making sure it finishes above the level of your head.

Outside block

1 Start in ready stance, with fists clenched.

2 As you step forward, bring your left fist up to behind your ear and pull your right arm across your chest.

3 Chamber the right arm back, and bring the left blocking fist round just below eye level, making sure block finishes past the line of your head and body.

Downwards X block

1 Start in ready stance, with fists clenched.

2 As you step forward, chamber your fists slightly, then shoot your arms out to the front, crossing them just above the wrists. Make sure the block is below the level of your groin.

Rising X block

1 Start in ready stance, with fists clenched.

3 Keeping them crossed, shoot the block to above the level of your head.

2 As you step forwards, cross your forearms in front of your chest.

Blocking with a partner

The blocking drills featured here are very important for your development as a *karateka*. Not only will they improve your timing but they will also help you get used to actual contact with an opponent.

Starting position

Pair off with somebody of approximately the same size and weight – who knows how to punch – and stand in front of each other, in opposing front stances, at just outside an arm's length apart. Your partner will punch and you will apply the appropriate or designated block – your partner can call out which block he wants you to perform. Carry out the exercise slowly to start with, stopping in between each move, then work up speed, or make the attack and defence moves continuous, as you increase in proficiency.

> **must know**
> If you follow your block with a reverse punch it will better prepare you for sparring as it will start to become a habit.

Downwards block
The forearm should make contact around the inside of your opponent's elbow, and as you knock his arm away he will be opened up and vulnerable to a quick reverse punch (see page 116).

Rising block
The contact should be made just below the opponent's wrist, rolling his punch over your head and putting you underneath his strike for your counterattack.

Outside block
Contact should be made with the outside of your opponent's arm, just above the elbow – this will give you the greatest leverage to unbalance him. As he is pushed round, he will not be able to use his other hand against you.

did you know?
Karate slippers are occasionally worn, especially when a student has a problem such as a foot infection. Ask your instructor if in any doubt.

Inside block
Contact is made midway between your opponent's wrist and elbow and it will turn your opponent slightly, leaving him open for a reverse punch.

Downwards X block
Try to catch the kick as close to the foot as possible, to give yourself the best chance of stopping it dead. From this position you could grab his foot as the start of your counterattack.

Rising X block

Make sure the X of your X block is higher than the top of your head. If your opponent has a weapon it should be relatively easy to twist it out of his hands using this block.

want to know more?

• Take it to the next level and perform blocks as part of a sequence of moves, as in the *katas* on page 164.

• The blocks shown are the basics, to learn more advanced methods ask your instructor or study a book such as *Essentials of Wado-ryu Karate* by Chris Thompson (Paul H. Crompton Ltd.)

6 The punches

Kicking may be more powerful, more
spectacular and more likely to find favour
with competition judges, but it has a downside.
Kicks are slower than punches and if you are
not an expert, they are more likely to get you
into trouble. No good *karateka* will neglect his
hand technique, and beginners shouldn't either
– all your offensive techniques should involve
sharp, powerful punches. As this section
shows, well-executed punches can be as
devastating as almost any kick.

Punching

There are numerous hand strikes used in most forms of karate – punches, knife-hand strike, back fist, palm heel, and so on – but for now we are going to concentrate on two variations of straightforward punching.

Technique

Hand strikes, notably punches, are a huge part of karate's offensive technique, as they can be delivered speedily and stealthily in sparring situations. This last part is especially useful to an inexperienced *karateka*, since if you are not yet super quick it's likely your opponent will spot your intention to kick as you set up to carry out the move. Therefore in any good karate club, all grades will continue to work on their punching technique with as much diligence as they apply to kicks.

When punching, the emphasis will be on delivering an effective strike through speed and accuracy rather than sheer power. And since even the best punch will rarely have the strength of a properly executed kick, they are more useful for point scoring in competition, wearing an opponent down, or launching surprise attacks. Hence punching practice will not be aimed at developing sheer power. Indeed, when punching, smaller lighter *karateka* can have a considerable advantage over bigger, more cumbersome opponents because of their speed of movement. Nor will they be sacrificing power, as elementary physics dictates that a fast punch delivered by a light body can contain more force on impact than a physically stronger punch with a slower movement. Think of your punching arm as a striking snake: fast, fluid and effective.

When punching, strength of hand and forearm is as important as strength of upper arm and shoulder. A strengthened hand and forearm will hold the wrist steady, and so the punching fist will remain straight and true as the blow lands. Practising punching against resistance equipment (see box below) will help build up this strength, but the real work will be done on the *dojo* floor – in press-ups. Press-ups on fingertips or clenched fists (see page 36) are the best and simplest method of strengthening your punching. The clenched fist method will be particularly effective – especially if you push your hands off from the floor – as it will help you get used to making contact with your knuckles. However, always make sure you are clenching your fist correctly (see Fists of fury, page 112), or you could damage your hands on a hard floor.

For maximum impact, as the punch lands your opposite arm should be chambered back.

The makiwara

In many *dojos*, a punchbag hung from overhead is used for punching practice, but traditionally, *karateka* worked out on a piece of equipment called a makiwara. This is a tapered wooden or bamboo post, about 2.5 metres (8 feet) in length, with the narrower end set at least 1 metre (3 feet) into the ground. The top, at around shoulder level, is 12 cm (5 in) across and bound with straw to form padding down the first 30 cm (11¾ in). This section is used as a target for punches and kicks.

Makiwaras remain popular in today's karate, although they are now constructed with integral stands and are made from plywood with foam rubber padding. (See also page 152.)

Fists of fury

The karate fist is nothing like a boxing fist or a normal fist, and, again unlike boxing, you have no protection on your fist – you can't even build up a shielding layer of muscle. This means it is crucial you form your fist correctly or you could injure your hands. Your fist must be closed tightly and held in such a way that it can deliver the most effective blow, but at the same time afford itself the greatest degree of protection.

To form the correct fist:

1 Hold your hand out flat, palm upwards, thumb pointing out.

2 Fold your fingers tightly down on themselves so the tips touch where their bases meet the palm. Thumb remains extended.

3 Roll fingers towards you so tips dig into palm, then fold thumb tightly across middle part of first two fingers.

4 Extend arm straight out with palm facing down, and a straight line along the forearm and back of the hand. The line of the inner forearm along the inside of the hand should be virtually straight, too.

The straight lines of the arm and the hand are for strength on impact, but the inner arm line is doubly important because if that is correct the first two knuckles will be pushed forwards. This is crucial for karate punching, since these two knuckles are supported by the forearm, whereas the other two aren't and could easily get broken if used for striking.

must know

A strong stance is vital both before and after executing the step in a step and punch. As you start the move, the strong stance will allow you to push forwards with real power, while stopping the step firmly means that you can get the most leverage with your hips to power up the punch.

Four rules of punching

1 Focus: Concentrate the power of your punch into your fist and don't dissipate the movement's energy or your mental focus anywhere else.

2 Target: Direct your punch at one of the two main target areas – solar plexus or head – and stick to that; don't aim vaguely and don't try to change your mind mid-punch.

3 Carry on: Even if you can see your opponent moving to block your punch, continue with it – don't attempt to pull it or redirect it. Assume the speed and power of your punch will get past any attempts to block it.

4 Pull away: Whether it has landed on target or not, once your punch has snapped into its strike, pull your arm back with the same sort of speed as you landed the blow. To leave your arm extended for too long will leave you very open to a counterattack.

Chamber your punches

Just as we discussed in the previous section that blocking was a chamber action and must have a balancing movement on the other side, so it is with punching. When one fist punches, the other returns to the ready position, tucked in just above the belt, with palm facing upwards, poised to block or punch. This chambering action should be as swift and as forceful as the punch.

Basic punching technique

There is a lot more to karate punching technique than simply flinging your fist out at your opponent. Broken down into its component parts, the technique comprises four different elements coordinated into one fluid movement.

must know
Aim at a spot 5–7.5 cm (2–3 in) behind your target; that way you will be compensating for your opponent starting to move backwards.

Feet and movement

Just as a big tree will have strong roots, so the basis of any punches will be your stance – hand strikes are no different from blocks or any other karate move in this respect. In order to give your punch maximum strength both your feet should be firmly planted on the ground as it lands – this will enable you to push all the way up through your legs. This means that if you are moving forwards or backwards as you punch, your arms and legs must be in total coordination. As your feet move into the step, your punching arm should be starting its movement; this will maximize your forward momentum. The timing of the punch should be such that it reaches its target a split second after the step has been completed.

Corkscrew motion

The main difference between a karate punch and a boxing punch is how the fist travels from its poised position to its target. In boxing, for defensive purposes, fists are usually held with palms facing inwards and most punches are landed with them in the same position, hence the fist travels straight. In karate, because the fist starts palm upwards as it tucks in by the waist, then makes contact with the palm facing down, it screws around through

180 degrees. It's this twist that will give a straight punch added power and make it much more difficult to block. The fist should complete this twisting movement with a sharp snap to concentrate the force of the punch.

Hip rotation

As you perform any karate hand strike, the hips will rotate into the movement to provide huge added power. This is the same for punching while stepping or standing still – while pushing up from the soles of the feet, the hip will twist towards the punching arm, snapping to coordinate with the snapping of the arm. This rotation transmits power and, by focusing it into one sharp movement, magnifies the push coming up through the legs. So if you are punching with the right hand, rotate your hips to the right, and the other way around for the left.

Breathing and relaxation

As you move into your strike you should be breathing out. This push of air from your lungs should be coordinated with your attacking movement, and therefore needs to be sharp and powerful, culminating in a fearsome *kiai* (or yell) to give vent to your inner spirit as you make your strike. This also has the advantage of your lungs being empty in case you are stepping into a counterattack. As you are making your move, your entire body should be relaxed, tensing only at the moment of impact, as you yell your *kiai*. This is because you need to be rigid to impart the power of your punch, but to tense your arms or legs before that point will impede the speed of your movement.

must know

To achieve maximum impact, make sure your punches land with a fully straightened arm and a locked elbow.

Reverse punch (*Gyaki-zuki*)

This is one of the most powerful and effective hand strikes in any *karateka*'s arsenal. It is so-called because it is a punch thrown with the hand opposite to the leading leg – left foot forwards, right reverse punch, and vice versa.

The reverse punch is a move greatly favoured in sparring, since it is a natural and immediate follow-up to a well-delivered block. Also, because it pushes directly up from the back leg, which should be straight if you are in a front stance, the power gained from the snapping of the hips as you land the punch will be greater.

The movement of the reverse punch begins from a front stance with the leading hand (left) extended over the leading knee (also left) – approximately a downwards block position – and the punching hand nestled just above the belt. The feet stay still, or might twist slightly as the hips snap, and the right hand shoots out from the hip. Aiming for the opponent's solar plexus, the arm should remain parallel to the floor, with any adjustment for reduction in height being taken up by a lowering of the stance. This allows the fist to shoot straight out, beginning its corkscrew twist as the elbow passes the body, which is roughly halfway through the movement.

As the body tenses as the punch lands, the hips have snapped round, being pushed by a straight back leg. The arm is straight and rigid, the hips are pushed forwards and the body is upright with the shoulders square-on.

must know

A reverse punch is often known as a counter punch because it is such a reliable technique for leading a counterattack after a block.

- Front stance.
- Left fist over leading knee.
- Opposite fist (right) ready to strike.
- Body upright, shoulders and hips turned slightly.

Start position

Final position
(front view)

Final position
(side view)

- Opposite fist out with straight arm.
- Leading fist chambered back to belt.
- Back leg straight.
- Hips snapped round, shoulders turned the other way, body upright.

Lower reverse punch (*Gedan-gyaki-zuki*)

The lower reverse punch is an excellent counterattack, especially on a taller opponent. It can get under their guard and is often a complete surprise, since few competitors expect punches to be coming from that low.

For directing a reverse punch below your opponent's solar plexus – to the stomach or groin – make sure your front stance is low. Don't attempt to punch downwards from an upright stance or lean forwards with your hips pushed back. If you do this it will put you off balance, leaving you very vulnerable to counterattack, and your punch will lack strength, as you will not be able to make use of the power pushed up from your legs and hips. Simply get lower in your stance and punch straight.

1 The stance is still a front stance, but it is slightly longer and the hips are lowered. The body remains upright.

2 The stance remains at that height, and the punch will connect with a lower target, but the arm will be straight out from the shoulder and thus will not lose any power.

Upper reverse punch (*Age-gyaki-zuki*)

This is another effective counterattack, and one that can be delivered with maximum strength.

To direct a reverse punch at an opponent's head level, you will always (unless he's tiny) be punching at an upward angle. For fully effective punching, you should slightly lower your stance and increase that angle, which will ensure that you can drive your blow upwards with all the speed and strength generated by your legs and hips.

However, as each reverse punch – middle, upper and lower – is delivered with the punching fist in the same starting position, your chamber action will not be affected by the intended height of the punch.

1 The stance is still a front stance, but the hips are slightly lowered and the body remains upright.

2 The stance remains at that height, and the punch is angled upwards to draw maximum power from the legs and hips.

Lunge punch (*Oi-zuki*)

This coordinated step-and-punch is a real staple of *kata* and sparring. The opposite of the reverse punch, this time the punch is thrown by the same hand as the leading leg.

This movement begins in a front stance, with your left leg forwards, your left fist above your knee, and your right fist tucked in just above your belt. As the forward step commences, raise your left fist so your arm is extended in front of the middle of your chest, this will serve as protection and will 'sight' your punch. Begin the movement – corkscrewing your right hand forwards – as your right foot comes level with your left in the step. The timing should be so that your punch lands a fraction after the step is complete and your right foot is firmly planted on the floor. It is at that point that the hips can snap round in coordination with the fist snapping into the punch.

In a move such as this, getting the step right is as crucial as the technique for the punch itself, since the power for the blow should start to generate as soon as the back foot starts to move forwards. The snapping round of the hips then increases that power and it is this force that drives on into the snap of the punch.

Be careful not to let your forward momentum and punching action cause your body to lean forwards. It will momentarily throw you off balance.

must know
As with the reverse punch, all muscles should be relaxed when the lunge punch is thrown,and simultaneously tensed when the punch lands.

- Front stance.
- Leading fist over leading knee.
- Opposite fist ready to strike.
- Body upright, shoulders and hips turned slightly.

Start position

Final position
(side view)

Final position
(front view)

- Leading leg has changed as step has been completed.
- Punch is straight out from shoulder.
- Other fist is chambered back to belt.
- Hips snapped round, shoulders turned the other way and body is upright.

must know

Because of the step forwards that is part of the lunge punch, during sparring it is a very useful method of closing down the distance between you and your opponent.

Lower lunge punch (*Gedan-oi-zuki*)

Like the lower reverse punch, this is also an effective surprise attack, as it is a lower-than-expected punch.

To lunge punch below your opponent's chest, angle your fist downwards as it corkscrews out and lower your stance by dropping your hips and taking a slightly longer step. If your body does not remain upright as you step, the lower lunge punch will leave you even more susceptible to losing your balance than the reverse punch.

1 As with the reverse punch, the stance is still a front stance, but it is slightly longer and the hips are lowered. The body remains upright.

2 The step comes through with the head remaining at the same level, so the stance height doesn't change and the punch will be angled downwards to still connect with the lower target area.

Upper lunge punch (*Age-oi-zuki*)

A fast, effective and powerful move that will often
surprise an opponent.

The theory behind the upper lunge punch is the
same as with the upper reverse punch (see page 119)
– because you need to punch upwards, you need to
set your stance a bit lower to punch with added
power. Also, remaining low as you step in on your
opponent increases the chances of getting under his
guard or his throwing himself off balance if he
attempts to counter downwards.

1 The stance is still a front stance, but
the hips are slightly lowered. The body
remains upright.

2 The stance remains at that height, and the
punch is aimed to connect with a target area
higher than the puncher's shoulder, but
balance and stance are still solid.

Punching drills

The following drills are designed as basic punching practice. They will help you to become familiar with the movements and increase speed and coordination.

Basic punching technique

This drill is for you to practise the basic technique of punching. Carried out from a riding stance, the punches can be in a central, lower or upper direction (see opposite), but will not be reverse or lunge, and there will be no stepping or moving of the feet. Thus you will be free of any distraction and can concentrate on the punching movement.

Take up a riding stance, feet shoulder width apart, knees flexed to slightly drop the hips. Extend one arm in front of your chest, with either a clenched fist or a knife hand, and tuck the other in, in a fist, next to your belt. Punch, with corkscrew motion, to where the other hand was extended level with your chest, as that hand comes back to the ready position at your hip. Although your shoulders will start and finish square-on, you will still snap your hips into the punch to give it extra power. Repeat the exercise, punching with the other hand.

Begin punching in slow motion, to ensure that you get the action absolutely right – you can still snap the punch at what would be the point of impact, since even though it is performed slowly it should still have power. Then raise the tempo to around half speed to establish a rhythm, before you perform a number of punches at full speed.

Start position
(front view)

Start position
(side view)

- For a central punch make sure you keep well balanced.
- Drop hips into stance.
- Shoulders should be turned slightly .

- Chamber right fist.
- Keep left punching arm level.

Final position for
a lower punch

Final position for
an upper punch

- The stance has to be dropped to put the shoulders closer in line with the target area.

- The stance stays at the same level to get greater leverage when punching upwards.

Reverse punch

It is impossible to properly practise a reverse punch from a riding stance, so this drill will be executed from a front stance and will involve stepping forwards between each punch. It is an important drill, as in so many sparring situations you will be performing a reverse punch *after* you have stepped into a move rather than during. For the step you make between each punch, you can either perform a block or simply make the step.

Start from a riding stance and step forwards into a front stance, with leading fist extended either over leading knee or held level with the chest. Shoulders and hips should be turned slightly; the other fist is in the chambered position. Without shifting the feet, use chambered fist to perform a reverse punch to chest level (see above opposite). The shoulders should be turned the other way and the body upright, and the hips should snap round as the punch snaps to its conclusion.

After punching, relax body into a regular front stance – pull the punching fist back and extend the other arm to correspond with the leading leg – and step forwards, changing your leading arm and leg. Perform a reverse punch with the other hand (see below opposite).

Once you have completed two punches, step backwards with what is your front leg, leaving that arm forward so you are now in a conventional front stance. Reverse punch. Step backwards again and reverse punch with the other hand.

Step forwards into a regular front stance, and repeat the drill.

> **must know**
> This drill should be practised with punches at all three heights – head, chest and groin – with the stance adjusted as necessary when you make the step.

First reverse punch

- Body upright and shoulders turned slightly.
- Leading fist opposite leading knee.
- Opposite fist chambered.

Second reverse punch

- The step has been made.
- The body is still upright and the shoulders turned the other way.
- The punch has been thrown level with the floor with the opposite hand.

Lunge punch with step

Unlike the previous two drills, which were either
static punching or stepping and then punching, the
lunge punch drill involves simultaneously stepping
and punching. All levels of *karateka* usually find it an
advantage to warm-up their punching techniques
with some riding stance punching before starting
step-and-punch drills.

Start from a conventional front stance, with leading
fist over leading knee and opposite fist chambered.
With leading arm still extended, raise it to chest level
and start to step forwards, keeping head at an even
height. As described on page 120, start the punching
movement as your feet cross midway during the
step, and, snapping your hips round, aim to 'land'
the punch at chest level and central to where your
opponent would be. You should finish in a strong
front stance, with the other hand forwards.

As soon as that first punch has snapped into place,
immediately repeat the move by starting another
step-and-punch, with what is now the leading arm
and leg. Then, when that second punch has landed,
repeat the movement twice, but step backwards this
time as you punch. After two such punches, you
should be back at the spot you started.

Start this exercise slowly, making sure all your
stances and moves are correct, then speed up so
that the two steps become one fluid sequence and
not two separate movements. If you have the space
wherever you are practising, add more steps to the
sequence so you are doing four or five punches in
each direction.

Start position

- Body upright and shoulders turned slightly.
- Leading fist over leading knee.
- Opposite fist chambered.

Final position

- The step has been made.
- The body is still upright and the shoulders turned the other way.
- The opposite arm and leg are now forward.

Punching and blocking drill

This is a drill to be practised with a partner of approximately the same height and weight; it combines the blocking drills (see page 98) with the reverse and lunge punch drills above.

Stand opposite each other, about an arm's length apart, one in a front stance and the other in a back stance. The *karateka* in the front stance steps forwards aiming a lunge punch at the other's chest; the other steps back into another back stance, blocking with either an inward or an outward block. Once the block has been completed, the blocker will use his chambered fist to deliver a reverse punch to the puncher's midsection, which will put them in a front stance. Both sides will then resume their original stances, but this time with the other leg and arm as lead, and repeat the drill using the opposite hands from the first moves.

After two such sequences have been completed in one direction, the roles and the directions will be reversed to allow each *karateka* the chance to practise punching and blocking. The drill should start slowly, in each direction, and then, as timing and confidence increase, it should speed up to slick, instinctive moves.

Spontaneous combinations

Different level punches and different blocks should be practised – lower punch and downwards block, upwards punch and rising block. These can either be pre-arranged between both partners or, once you get confident, as a spontaneous exercise.

must know
It is vital that the blocks make contact with the puncher's arm and physically knock it away, as this will teach you how much strength is really needed and what it feels like to make contact.

- Both stances are firm and strong.
- The block finishes outside the line of the blocker's body or head, making sure he cannot get hit.
- The blocker will be able to spot an opening for a counterattack.
- The blocked puncher should be aware he is particularly vulnerable to a reverse punch.

want to know more?
- To improve your punching techniques it is worth studying conventional boxing and how punches are thown in that discipline.
- Local boxing clubs will be found in *Yellow Pages* or in your council's sports and leisure listings,
- Phone up a local club and ask if you can go along to watch a couple of sessions.

weblink
www.boxinggyms.com

7 The kicks

Kicking is probably the reason most people take up karate in the first place, and being able to execute fast, powerful kicks will always be a spectacular achievement. They aren't easy though and kicking before you are ready, or kicking past your limit, will leave you open to counterattack in sparring, or may even result in serious injury. Therefore, as this section shows, it is vital for beginners to take it slowly when learning the full range of karate kicks.

Kicking

Kicks are the central plank of any karate training, and not simply because of their importance in sparring situations. Good kicking will involve movement and technique that isn't entirely natural for most students. It requires dedication and application to achieve the degree of strength and suppleness needed to master it.

must know
When starting to learn to kick, be careful not to overreach. Trying to kick too high too soon will greatly increase your risk of injury.

Flexibility, balance and speed

To learn to kick embodies the true spirit of learning karate. Karate kicks can be aimed in any direction, can strike at any height and can come at an opponent in a number of different ways, yet there is one thing they all have in common: to execute any kick effectively you need flexibility, balance and speed. To attain the flexibility needed to be able to deliver a kick at head height, stretching is of prime importance. Whereas the point of stretching as part of your warm-up is to get the blood flowing around your muscles and would be the same for any sport, stretching for kicking is much more specialized, and you are literally stretching muscles and ligaments to make them longer. Such an increase will make them looser, permitting kicks to be higher and faster.

Balance is vital for two reasons: because kicks are so much stronger than punches, the forward momentum generated will be greater, and the possibility of being carried past your vertical centre of gravity will increase accordingly; for most of your kicking movement you will be standing on only one foot, and therefore balance becomes doubly important. Good balance comes with increased control of your kicking action, and you will only attain that control through constant practice, which will lead to the increased strength and flexibility it requires.

The other direct result of muscle-stretching and practice is speed. The strength and flexibility you will gain will allow you to kick much faster, while the muscle memory you will attain through repetition means you'll start kicking instinctively instead of having to think what to do.

Kicking techniques

To learn to kick, you must learn some fundamental principles of body movement that will, after you have reached this point in your karate studies, simply seem like commonsense. However, they still need to be addressed when applied directly to kicking.

1 The body and head should remain as upright as possible throughout the kick's movement. Too often, especially with the back kick or side kick, an inexperienced *karateka* will not flex at the waist, which results in his head and shoulders dropping as the leg goes higher. This will not only put him off balance, but will also mean he will take longer to get back into a stance from which he can attack or defend competently, and he may well be forced to take his eyes off his opponent.

In the front snap kick the knee raises before the foot snaps up.

2 The hips will rotate into the kick. Just as you snap your hips into a punch or a block for added power, so you should snap your hips in the direction of the kick to add that bit extra on impact.

3 Retract your kicking foot as quickly as possible – you will not want your leg grabbed by your opponent,

especially if it is at shoulder height, since there is little you will be able to do to defend yourself. Also, withdrawing your foot and regaining your stance pulls your forward momentum up, allowing you to regain the distance you want from your opponent, and will keep the time spent on one foot to a minimum.

must know

Don't take your eyes off your opponent when kicking. Doing so will leave you vulnerable to counterattack.

4 Keep your standing foot flat on the floor with your standing leg slightly flexed at the knee. This is the nearest you will be able to get to a solid stance while one foot is in the air, and is for maximum stability and balance. It is important not to overreach your kick and go up on tiptoes, or lock the standing leg, leaving yourself less able to adjust your balance or absorb impact.

5 Don't forget your shoulders. Coordinating your shoulders to snap into the kick with your hips can give you a further power boost.

6 Keep your guard up. As your body remains as upright as possible, and the shoulders rotate into the kick, try to keep your lead fist extended and your opposite fist chambered during the kick. This will mean you have maximum protection and are poised to follow up the kick with a punch or a reverse punch.

These rules are relevant to all karate kicking, even though there are several different types of kick. The two most basic techniques – snap kicks (*geri-keage*) and thrust kicks (*geri-kekomi*) – are the ones we will be looking at in this section; each has a different action and different consequence for the kicker, thus should be used in different circumstances.

Thrust kicks

As the name might suggest, thrust kicks thrust out straight, as parallel as possible with the floor, and make contact with a pushing motion. They are not unlike punches in how they work, as they land with the leg locked out straight and they remain at the point of impact after the blow has landed. Thrust kicks can deliver more power in this pushing motion and, as the leg is completely extended, they are more effective if the kicking range is greater. But the downsides are that, since your foot remains in the target area for longer, you are vulnerable to leg grabs by your opponent, and the impact from the kick will transmit itself back into your body and may affect your balance. Thrust kicking can be applied to front kicks, side kicks and back kicks.

Snap kicks

Once again, the name is a giveaway – snap kicks snap out quickly from the knee to make contact, then the foot is retracted as soon as it has struck. Snap kicks are faster than thrust kicks, but won't deliver as much power; they also have a shorter reach and thus are more suitable if your opponent is closer. Because the foot is withdrawn as soon as it has made contact, only a minimal amount of shock from its landing on your target will be transmitted back to the kicker. This action will thus lessen the likelihood of any jolting upsetting your balance. Also, it will be more difficult for your opponent to grab your leg to start a counterattack and, as the snapping back of the foot reverses the move's momentum, it is easier to resume a stance for the next phase of the attack.

When the leg snaps outwards it should be perfectly straight.

The pros and cons of kicking

Arguments rage in *dojos* around the world as to whether kicking or punching will serve you better either on the sparring mat or in a fight situation. So, in the true spirit of diplomacy, we present the case for each side:

Pros:

• Nearly everybody's legs are longer than their arms and, therefore, well-placed kicks will ensure that an opponent keeps their distance from you.

• Strength – under normal circumstances a kick will be stronger than a punch, since leg muscles are considerably larger than arm muscles.

• Kicks look so spectacular, and other karate students know how difficult they are, that simply to be able to pull them off will unnerve and often intimidate an opponent.

• In a street fight situation there will be an enormous element of surprise working in your favour if you pull off a fast, powerful head-height kick.

Cons:

• The larger leg muscles will be more cumbersome, and thus kicking will not be as fast as punching.

• The higher a kick has to go – i.e. to head height – the longer it will take to get there, whereas a punch's starting position is already halfway there.

• No matter how fast your kicking is, you will be standing on one foot at some point, and that is when you are at your most vulnerable to counterattack.

• A badly executed kick, or one that doesn't come off, will hugely boost your opponent's confidence.

When executing a kick, never take your eyes off your opponent.

Be adaptable

Under any circumstances, the best kicks are the simplest,
and straightforward attacks are usually liable to be the most
effective. Keeping your moves simple will often mean adapting
them slightly to suit whatever situation you find yourself in.
One of the reasons karate students learn so many different kicks
at different heights is so they can, literally, think on their feet
and have something with which to carry out their attack at that
particular time. Also, this large repertoire of different techniques
will allow you to borrow an aspect from one to use in another
move to make it more efficient. So while you will have to learn
the kicks in classic karate style, once you've mastered them you
will be a far more dangerous opponent if you are prepared to
deviate from the true technique when necessary.

Feet apart

To carry out karate's kicking repertoire, each foot will have to use a number of different striking areas. Which kick requires which particular striking area will have a relevance as to which kick you decide to use under which circumstances. This is because your opponent's target areas will vary as to how hard they are and not all of the foot's striking areas will be able to cope with all of them. The striking areas needed for the techniques in this section are as follows:

Ball of the foot (*koshi*) – front kicks and roundhouse kicks

To strike with the ball of the foot, the toes are pulled up and back as far as possible and the foot is either pointed (front kick) or pulled back at a right angle to the shin (roundhouse kick).

The ball of the foot will be your hardest and most effective striking surface and can be used on virtually anything.

Instep (*haisoku*) – front kicks

The foot is pointed and the toes are turned down; this will only usually be used for front kicks directed at the groin.

Because the foot contains so many fragile bones, and several are close to the instep's surface, it should not be used to attack hard targets such as the head.

Outside edge (*sokutu*) – side kicks

The foot is pointed and turned inwards, with the big toe drawn up and the others straight. The foot will be tensed to create a knife-edge along the outer side.

Not as vulnerable as the instep, but the bone running along the outside of the foot has very little natural protection, and therefore it should not be used to attack hard targets.

Heel (*kakoto*) – back kick

The foot is pointed and turned in, with the big toe drawn up and the others straight, similarly to the side kick, but the action of the kick will mean the heel is pushed forwards as the striking surface. In some cases – if it is being aimed particularly high – the heel will be used for a side kick strike.

Like the ball of the foot, the heel is very tough and can be used to strike the hardest of target areas.

When executing a front kick, pull the toes back to strike with the ball of the foot.

Front snap kick (*Mae-geri-keage*)

The simplest and most used of all karate's kicks, the front snap kick can be aimed at the groin, body or head and is a fast, effective method for scoring points or keeping your opponent at a distance.

Starting from a front stance with the left leg forwards, the right leg moves up and forwards, bending at the knee until the foot is just past the left knee. At that point the right foot snaps out to make impact as the leg straightens and the hips are rotated forwards into the kick. As soon as the kick has landed, the knee bends again to snap the foot back to the position by the knee. The right leg then regains its forward momentum to plant the foot firmly on the floor in a front stance with the right leg forwards.

- Start from a strong front stance.
- Left fist is forwards with left leg.
- Right fist is chambered.

- From the front stance, bring the foot up to just above the opposite knee.
- Keep the body upright and shoulders turned slightly.
- Fist should be up to keep guard throughout the move.

- Foot snaps out to strike with either ball or instep, depending where kick is aimed.
- Hips rotate forwards into the kick.
- Body and hands remain in roughly the same position.
- As soon as it has struck, the foot is withdrawn to a safer distance.

Side snap kick (*Yoko-geri-keage*)

The side snap kick is a difficult kick to perfect, but it will reward that effort, as it is one of the most spectacular looking and powerfully explosive kicks in the repertoire. It can be delivered from a side stance or a front stance, to any height target, and will come up quickly to surprise your opponent.

From a front stance

The big difference between this and the previous kick is that as the rear foot comes up with the knee bent, the hips and body rotate in a way that turns the heel of the standing foot towards the target. This means that in order to face forwards you will be looking over your right shoulder.

As the foot comes up with the knee bent, the leg is turned sideways so that the outside of the leg and foot are on top and the thigh and lower leg are as close to the same level as possible, parallel with the floor. The standing foot will be halfway to turning the heel towards the target. From this position the hips continue to rotate, the standing foot turns all the way and the foot snaps out with the edge striking the target. The right arm will be extended parallel with the leg for balance, and the body remains as upright as possible. After the strike the foot is immediately withdrawn to the previous bent knee position and the body is rotated back to square-on as you step down into a front stance with the right leg forwards.

must know

When you practise side snap kicks, alternate with your front and back foot. A side snap kick from the front foot will be very useful in sparring.

- Start in a conventional strong front stance.

- As the foot comes up, it is turned to the side and raised up towards the same level as the knee.
- The body and hips are turning to accommodate this.
- The standing foot has started to turn its heel towards the target.

- The foot thrusts out, side-on, striking with the edge.
- The standing foot has completed its turn.
- The body is as upright as possible; you will be able to see over your shoulder.
- The arm is extended for balance and protection.

- As the foot withdraws after the strike, the body and standing foot start turning back.
- Fists remain raised for protection as you step back down into a front stance.

From a side stance

A side kick from a side stance is a very useful technique for sparring, since you are likely to be in that stance because it presents the narrowest target to your opponent. Unlike the other kicks in this section, it is performed with the leading leg, indicating that it is a very fast manoeuvre.

Step sideways in a side stance, bringing the leg furthest from your target up next to the kicking leg – this starts your momentum. Raise the kicking leg, bending the knee, as you would from the front stance; the difference is that the hips, body and standing foot will already be halfway through the necessary turn. Snap the foot out to strike with the edge and return to the bent knee position. Bring foot down on to the floor as the front foot of a strong side stance.

must know

Be very careful not to cross your feet when you make this step, as there will be too great a chance of your feet getting tangled up.

● From a side stance, bring the back foot up next to the front foot.
● Keep the body side-on and fists raised for protection.

● Bring the front foot up, bending the knee.
● The hips and body are half turned.

- Strike with edge of foot.
- Hips have completed their rotation, body is as upright as possible.
- Standing foot is fully turned with heel facing target.

- Step down into a side stance with kicking foot still in front.
- Withdraw foot immediately after strike.
- Hips, body and standing foot return to previous bent knee position.

Back thrust kick
(*Ushiro-geri-kekomi*)

This is a powerful kick that is particularly effective against an opponent who is behind you, or if you have been turned around by a previous manoeuvre.

From a front stance, pull your back foot up level with the front knee, but to the side of it. As you do so, look over the same shoulder as the raised knee. Thrust the raised foot out powerfully behind you, toes turned downwards so you are striking with the heel, aiming at the centre of your opponent's body. Keep looking over your shoulder, while your body remains as upright as possible and the heel of the standing foot points towards the target. Retract the foot as soon as it strikes and plant it back on the floor in the same front stance as when you started. Only now do you turn and start looking towards the front.

- Turn away from leading leg.
- Look over shoulder at target.

- Thrust your foot straight out, pushing it into centre of opponent's body.
- Turn your toes downwards to strike with heel.
- Keep your body as upright as possible.
- Keep looking over your shoulder.

- Withdraw foot as soon as strike has been made.
- Carry on looking over your shoulder.

- Turn to look back to the front as your foot lands and you are back in the same front stance.

Roundhouse kick (*Mawashi-geri*)

The roundhouse kick is fast, devastatingly powerful and versatile enough to be used against any part of your opponent's body, from the head down to the knee. It is a difficult move for the beginner, but it is vital to persist with it, as it can become one of the most effective strikes in your repertoire.

From the front stance, the back leg comes up turned over to the side, as it does for the side kick – the standing foot is starting to turn, the body remains upright. From here the foot comes around on a horizontal or angled arc, rather than snapping straight out, as the standing foot pivots to point at the target, so the hips will rotate completely, allowing the leg to come over and around. The strike is made with the instep or the toes are pulled back and it is made with the ball of the foot. The hands can clenched fists or knife hands. As soon as the strike has been made, the leg withdraws and steps forward as the leading leg in a front stance.

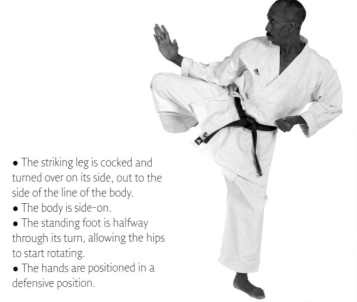

● The striking leg is cocked and turned over on its side, out to the side of the line of the body.
● The body is side-on.
● The standing foot is halfway through its turn, allowing the hips to start rotating.
● The hands are positioned in a defensive position.

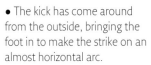

- The kick has come around from the outside, bringing the foot in to make the strike on an almost horizontal arc.
- The standing foot has turned so that the heel points to the target.
- The hips have rotated completely to allow the leg to turn.
- The body is still as square-on and upright as possible.
- Following the strike the foot should return to the cocked position.

- The hips and standing foot rotate back into place.
- The hands are kept in a protective position.
- The kicking foot has stepped down to the floor to become the lead leg in a front stance.

Kicking drills

Practising individual kicking drills is the best way to learn the art of kicking. You should perform these exercises from a riding stance (see page 66).

(see page 66)

must know

Your hand position may be varied from riding stance to riding stance depending on what you are going to do next.

Building control

The first and most basic kicking drill is to perform the kicks you have learned from a riding stance, without moving up and down the *dojo*. Although the preceding pages described the kicks as being part of a forwards stepping move, this exercise will allow you to concentrate purely on the motion of the kick, building up control of all aspects of the move without forward momentum carrying you through. It will help you attain a good understanding of how each kick works.

Perform these drills by kicking with alternate legs, returning to a riding stance in between each move. Start slowly, making sure you get the movement right, then gradually increase your speed.

Use of equipment

Many clubs will use heavy punching bags or makiwaras (see page 111) for practice kicking. Be very careful when starting out and kicking against a piece of equipment as it will not move if your kick is obviously going wrong. Beginners should be supervised when using this equipment. Talk to your instructor first.

Kicking on a heavy bag will get you used to making contact.

Front kick

1 Start in riding stance.

2 Bring the knee up to the middle of your body. Do not straighten your stance and make sure the standing leg remains slightly bent.

3 Snap the kick out from there. Your head should remain at the same height throughout the move.

Side kick

1 Start in riding stance.

2 Bring the kicking foot up, starting to rotate the hips over, and turn the standing foot so that the bent leg can turn over on to a horizontal plane.

3 Snap the foot out, fully rotating the hips and with the standing foot finishing its turn to point the heel towards the target. Strike with the edge of the foot.

NB Retract the foot as soon as the strikes have been made, and return to the riding stance.

Back kick

1 Start in the riding stance, look over your shoulder at your target.

2 Still looking, bend your knee to bring your foot up in front of you.

3 Thrust the foot back to strike with the heel, keeping your body as upright as possible and continuing to look behind you.

NB Once the kick has landed, retract the foot to the position in front of you – continuing to look behind you – and step back into riding stance.

Roundhouse kick

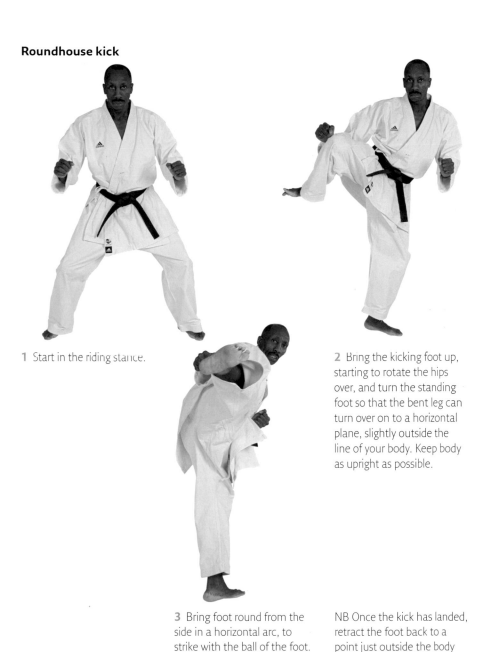

1 Start in the riding stance.

2 Bring the kicking foot up, starting to rotate the hips over, and turn the standing foot so that the bent leg can turn over on to a horizontal plane, slightly outside the line of your body. Keep body as upright as possible.

3 Bring foot round from the side in a horizontal arc, to strike with the ball of the foot. The hips will be fully rotated to facilitate this movement.

NB Once the kick has landed, retract the foot back to a point just outside the body line and step back into the riding stance.

Drills with a partner

This kicking practice will make kicks part of a forwards stepping move as described earlier. Having a partner block them will provide some idea of actual contact.

Pair up with somebody of approximately your height and weight and take a front stance in front of him, while he assumes a back stance. You should be about 1.5 metres (5 feet) apart. You will be advancing, kicking at your partner who will be blocking with the appropriate move. After you have taken two steps forwards, performing the same kick with each foot, switch stances (you in back stance, he in front stance) and you block as he kicks at you with each foot. Perform prearranged kicks to begin with, then as you get more confident try some gentle freestyling.

Front snap kick countered with an upwards block

Side kick countered with an inside block

Back kick met with a downwards block

Roundhouse kick countered with an outside block

want to know more?
• To improve your kicking technique, join a karate club. If you want to practise kicking in 'live' situations, look for one that puts particular emphasis on sparring and competition fighting.
• There are many different karate organizations that will be glad to help you search for a local club, a list of these can be found on pages 186–7.

weblinks
• For a regularly updated list of clubs and organizations visit: www.dmoz.org
• And for clubs , organizations and equipment, visit: www.sportfocus.com

8 *Kata* and sparring

This final technique section is where we are going to put it all together and learn sequences of moves. These will considerably enhance your basic skills, as you will be carrying out the movements under genuine conditions so balance will be critical. They will also help you improve your ability to follow one move with another automatically. This is a vital part of sparring, as you will be able to attack and defend without having to think about it.

Kata

A *kata* is a prescribed series of karate movements: blocks, kicks and punches, each with its own name, performed against an imaginary opponent or opponents. Each *kata* is a sequence that could be described as a make-believe fight, but it will be of far greater significance to your training regime than that.

The philosophy of *kata*

Kata, translated, means 'form', and every karate style will have its own choreographed set pieces as a large part of its training programme – indeed, practically every other martial art has its own *kata*, although the Korean and Chinese styles will call them something different. In Japanese karate there are two types of *kata*: Shorin and Shorei. Shorin *kata* tend to be fast and agile, while Shorei put the emphasis on strength and power. Across the different styles of karate there are approximately 100 different *kata*, most consisting of between 20 and 50 moves. Because *kata* will be part of every level of karate training, the moves involved will require varying degrees of skill, from basic blocking and punching to complicated kicking and striking procedures. *Karateka* of all belts will learn *kata* as part of whatever grading they are aiming for, and it is not unusual for higher grades to have to remember and be expected to perform *kata* learned early in their studies.

Kata is usually assumed to be imaginary fighting – a series of 'air shots' – and is fiercely criticized in some quarters as being unrealistic, useless in a genuine combat situation thanks to its rigid formulae, and a distraction from the real business of karate training. But the reasons for the emphasis on *kata* are far more subtle than simply sparring with an imaginary opponent. Because so much of learning karate is the technical aspect, *kata* is where this is perfected and how your instructor will be able to judge how you are progressing. Also, each *kata*'s sequence will have been carefully constructed to put the *karateka* through a series of manoeuvres that will test his technique, balance, movement, timing and vision. By its very nature, this is something that will not necessarily replicate a realistic sparring session, as too often in competition, moves will be limited by what is most effective in that instance, and changes in direction will be minimal. *Kata* can be written to include turns, upward and downward moves and attacks and defences in all four directions that will, in essence, prepare the student for anything. It is by practising these sequences, which require a massive degree of mental and physical agility, that the student can be prepared for just about anything.

Many karate clubs stage public *kata* demonstrations to illustrate the prowess of their students as part of campaigns to attract new members – to see an entire class performing even a basic *kata* in perfect unison is a powerful sight.

Understanding *kata*
Simply performing *kata* will not be enough. It will not be enough to gain everything available from your training, and not be enough to get closer to the spirit of karate and what it means. *Kata* is something that must be *understood* by every student who hopes to progress to the best of their ability – often a teacher will ask a *karateka* for their interpretation of a *kata*

must know
When performing *kata*, execute each move with the strength and focus you would use if you were sparring. Don't slack off just because there is no opponent in front of you.

they are learning, to ensure that they know it is more than just a complicated dance.

Kata's roots are in the karate of 17th-century Okinawa, when the Satsumas banned the practising of martial arts, and training had to be done in secret. *Kata* were developed as an important part of the peasants' secret martial arts routines, since they provided the necessary all-over aerobic conditioning, tuned reflexes and kept muscle memories sharp. And since *kata* could be practised alone at any time of the day or night, they also meant people could learn how to deal with attack and rehearse combat techniques when regular sparring sessions weren't possible. Informal sequences were practised at this point, but it was universally understood that this was the best training method, and they developed into the specified series of movements we learn today, 300 years later, when karate has been sanctioned. What survives from those early days of secrecy, however, is the seriousness with which *kata* must be approached and the knowledge that rather than simply throwing a few moves, you are attacking and defending for your life.

It is this direct connection with karate's past through *kata* that will help students understand what they are learning, and the 'interpretation' they might be asked to give relates back to this. If you are performing, for instance, the Pinan Shodan *kata* (the most basic Shotokan *kata* and one demonstrated on page 164) and the sequence calls for a turn to the right and a downwards block, you may be asked 'What are you doing?' You will be expected to provide a scenario of how you were being attacked and why you made such a response. Of course, your

did you know?

Performing *kata* can bring its own range of aches. Taking supplements of cod liver oil and glucosamine regularly will go a long way towards easing joint pains, especially among older *karateka*.

interpretation might be different from that of the student next to you, but that doesn't matter as long as you have an understanding of why you are doing what you are doing.

It's precisely this understanding that means as you perform your moves you will do so as in a genuine combat situation – that the opponent you are blocking and punching is there in front of you. It will keep you and your karate sharp and ensure that you are getting the absolute most out of your training.

Kata **will help you realise karate's true potential.**

Pinan Shodan ('the first level of the peaceful mind')

The first and most basic of karate's *kata*, Pinan Shodan is ideal to achieve the right *kata* mindset through practice. The eight sequences of moves turn you in all directions as if facing multiple opponents. In some moves the hands are held in the knife-hand position as opposed to the clenched fist – see box.

1 Start in the ready stance.

2 Look left.

3 Turn 90 degrees to the left, starting a downwards block.

4 Step into a front stance completing the downwards block (see pages 88–9).

5 Step forwards with a right-hand mid-level punch.

6 Look over your right shoulder.

Knife-hand knowledge

The knife-hand block (see step 32, page 169) in this *kata* is the same movement as the clenched-fist inside block, but the hand is held straight with fingers slightly curled to tense them and the thumb held just apart. The palm is angled forwards at completion.

7 Turn 180 degrees ...

8 ... into a right front stance with a downwards block.

9 Pull back front foot into a cat stance, withdrawing right fist to shoulder level.

10 Strike the right fist out in an anti-clockwise motion to an eye-level strike.

11 Rotate the right fist into a mid-level punch.

12 Step forwards with a left-hand mid-level punch.

13 Look and turn to the left, pulling left foot back ...

14 ... to step forwards on it into a front stance, with a left-hand downwards block.

15 Step forwards on right foot ...

16 ... with a right-hand clenched-fist rising block.

17 Step forwards with a left-hand rising block.

18 Step forwards with a right-hand rising block and *kiai*.

19 Look to the left and turn 90 degrees to the right.

20 Step forwards into a left front stance ...

21 ... with a left-hand downwards block.

22 Step forwards with a right-hand mid-level punch.

23 Look over right shoulder and turn 180 degrees to the right.

24 Step forwards with a right-hand downwards block.

25 Step forwards with a left-hand mid-level punch.

26 Look to the left and turn 90 degrees to the left, pulling your left foot back.

27 Step forwards with a left-hand downwards block.

28 Step forwards with a right-hand mid-level punch.

29 Step forwards with a left-hand mid-level punch.

30 Step forwards with a right-hand mid-level punch and *kiai*.

31 Look over your left shoulder.

32 Pivot on your right foot, 180 degrees to your left, bringing your left foot round into a left cat stance, performing a right-hand downwards knife-hand block.

33 In the same stance, perform a left-hand downwards knife-hand block.

34 In the same stance, perform downwards twin knife hands (thrust hands out as for X block, but with backs of hands touching).

35 In the same stance, withdraw hands to right shoulder (the movement catches an opponent's kick then throws him off balance).

36 Return hands to guard position (left hand in front of face for protection, right hand chambered).

37 Look 45 degrees to the right.

38 Step forwards with a right-hand downwards knife-hand block.

39 In the same stance, perform downwards twin knife hands.

40 In the same stance, withdraw hands to left shoulder.

41 Return hands to guard position.

42 Look over your right shoulder and turn clockwise into a right-footed cat stance with a left-hand downwards knife-hand block.

43 In the same stance, perform a right-hand downwards knife-hand block.

44 In the same stance, perform downwards twin knife hands.

45 In the same stance, withdraw hands to left shoulder.

46 Return hands to guard position.

47 Look and turn to the left. Raise arms to fully rotate shoulders to relax.

48 Return to ready stance.

Sparring

As a beginner, you will not be sparring until you have mastered the basics of karate, and then only under strict supervision, but these are the basic guidelines.

When sparring always be prepared for an attack.

Block swiftly and strongly.

Get ready for a counter attack.

Stance

In any sparring contest, a large part of your success or failure will depend on how mobile you are; therefore, stances will be adapted for versatility and swift movement in any direction.

Although your feet will be in firm contact with the floor when you are landing a blow or a kick, while moving about the mat you will probably be up on the balls of your feet, with knees slightly bent, staying mobile and agile and able to drop into any more formal stance if required to do so.

Posture

Don't be tempted to lean backwards and forwards, as this will compromise your balance; try to keep your body as upright as possible at all times. Hold your head up straight with your chin tucked in. Hold your hands up in a guarding position with fists clenched, and stay relaxed until you actually make a strike – a relaxed body won't be hurt so much if it is hit and it will make all movement much easier.

Distance

When sparring, try to dictate the distance between you and your opponent, and to ensure that you keep that distance to outside his striking range. Not only will this keep you safe if your opponent is faster, but a slightly removed position will also give you a better overall view of anything he attempts.

Movement

Although you will be remaining relaxed and able to shift about the mat with agility, when you make an attacking move it should be sharp and direct. Glide across the mat, keeping your head at the same level, and avoid crossing your feet or even passing them too close to each other, as it will be too easy to get one caught up in your *gi*. Timing your moves is the secret to effective sparring.

Targets

In free sparring, any target below the belt or to your opponent's back or the back of the head will be off limits. As a beginner, for reasons of speed and accuracy, it will be better to aim for the body than the head, since the body is a bigger, closer target. Once you have decided on a target and started your move, don't attempt to change it, as that will give you problems with balance and power.

Contact

With the exception of full contact karate clubs, contact during sparring will be minimal. Kicks and punches to the head and face will be pulled before they land, but stopped close enough to let your opponent know they could have landed; blows to the body will usually land lightly, with enough power in them to make contact with the *gi*. Blocks are usually encouraged to land wholeheartedly, as they will need to be strong to divert the blow, and it is important you get used to what this contact feels like.

want to know more?

• There are many karate tournaments and competions around the UK, with *karateka* of all levels taking part. Talk to your instructor if you want to compete – he will tell you if you are ready or not.

• For more information about karate competitions, visit the Competition Karate Association at www.cka.org.uk

• To build your sparring skills practise two- or three-step sparring, which is designed to get beginners used to carrying out moves against an opponent but with the minimum risk of accident. Advanced karate books will carry details, or ask at your local club.

9 What next?

Having absorbed the philosophies, lessons and introductions to basic techniques, you are, no doubt, keen to progress. In this section, there is advice on how the karate grading system works, how best to progress and what to look for – and what to avoid – when looking for a club to join.

Choosing a karate club

A recent survey showed that for nearly half the people who had joined a karate club, it was the first one they had visited. No wonder that among new karate students the drop-out rate in the first six months is so high. There's more to finding the right karate club than a thumb through *Yellow Pages*.

must know

Clubs to avoid are clubs that:
• **Promise you a black belt too quickly.**
• **Want you to sign a contract committing you for a length of time.**
• **Put emphasis on sparring and fighting rather than on technique.**
• **Are not affiliated to any national or international organization.**

Consider all angles

Remarkably, two of the most important factors in your choice of club have nothing to do with karate or karate instruction: they are location and cost. Although we're not suggesting you choose a club just because it's convenient, if it's a pain to get to the chances are you'll miss lessons, and if it hasn't got showers then you don't want a long journey home. And as for cost, you have to be able to afford regular and frequent lessons if you want to progress.

Look for training facilities – changing rooms and showers included, if there are any – that seem safe, clean, well-lighted and with a regular temperature. Are adults and children training together? Although a family atmosphere is a plus point, children should not train alongside adults, since their needs will be so different. Then observe the class before it starts – much can be learned from watching the students arrive. Are they punctual? Do they bow to the *dojo*? Are they rowdy? Do they start warming up and practising before the instructor arrives? Are they respectful to each other, regardless of rank? Then, when the instructor arrives, how quickly does the class settle down? The teacher should command respect and exude authority without bullying, intimidating or flexing any ego. He shouldn't be without humour, though. Don't forget, this is supposed to be enjoyable.

Is there a good spread of belts throughout the club? If there are, this points to good progression, as a large proportion of lower *kyus* in a long-established club points to a lack of improvement, while too many black belts imply students are being rushed through gradings and not learning properly. This second point is not uncommon, as karate in the UK and the USA is pretty much unregulated and anybody can set up as a teacher and hand out gradings. Unscrupulous operators who promise to train newcomers to black belt in 18 months or two years have never been short of eager clientele. It should take between three and five years of regular training to reach that standard, and you should be suspicious of any teacher who promises one in much less time than that.

However, when, after visiting several clubs, you make the decision to join one, don't ignore your gut instinct. Whichever establishment gives off the best vibe – i.e. you simply feel most at home in – is probably the one for you.

must know

Karate is an ideal pastime for children, it teaches self-control, self-discipline and promotes physical and mental fitness. Karate clubs that accept children should provide separate classes from adults. And they should not take on children that are too young. Under the age of six or seven children do not have the motor skills necessary to learn karate. Be wary of a club that offers karate classes for toddlers' or very young children's karate.

Ten things you'll find in a good karate club

1 A calm, quiet atmosphere of mutual respect. It should be obvious that the students respect each other as well as the instructor and that the teacher respects them.

2 You will be made to feel welcome to watch an entire training session. The club should not appear to hide anything from you, and, as long as you don't get in anybody's way, make sure you are comfortable.

3 The club should lend you a *gi* for a 'try out' session (or let you wear a tracksuit) before you commit. No club should expect you to invest in any kit until you have decided whether or not karate is for you.

A good karate club will have a mix of belts and a strong spirit of togetherness.

4 Fees will be uncomplicated, with no contracts or extra 'enrolment' or 'subscription' payments. That is to say if you think you are being ripped off, you probably are.

5 Beginners and junior *kyus* will be constantly supervised. If it isn't the instructor himself, one of the senior belts should be doing this.

6 The teacher or a senior student answers all your questions. Don't be shy about asking – when you are in a new environment, there is no such thing as a stupid question.

7 The emphasis is on technique and *kata* over sparring and fighting. Although there ought to be some regular sparring, for a beginner the technique has to come first.

8 A good spread of different colour belts. This implies that the students are progressing steadily, and staying at the club long term.

9 The class warms up and cools down properly. This will greatly reduce their – therefore your – risk of injury.

10 The students and the instructor all seem to be happy. Never forget, you're supposed to be enjoying learning karate!

did you know?
The three things to remember in this process are: observe, discuss and be forearmed with knowledge. If you've read this book you've taken care of the latter, so go along and watch – more than once if you want to – and don't be afraid to ask questions.

Gradings

Although every karate style or organization will have a slightly different approach to gradings and the corresponding colours of belts, the thinking and essential requirements will be the same.

The belts

Kyu means the colour of the belt below black belt level. *Dan* is the term used for ranking at black belt level or above.

When you start learning karate, you will wear a white belt, symbolizing the beginner, or 10th *kyu*, and in most well-run clubs you will take your first grading to 9th *kyu* after about three months of regular training.

For your first grading (9th *kyu*) you will be expected to have gained an understanding of what karate is and how it works. You should have mastered the basic stances, blocking techniques and upwards and lower punches. You will not be expected to be particularly fast or strong at this point, and you will be judged on your balance, control and coordination. When you perform your *kata* you will be assessed on your combinations, on how each move flows into the next, and how effectively you perform each move when coming out of another. If you are required to spar at this first grading (you might not be), it will be very controlled and probably in short attack and defence bursts of two or three moves each.

As you move up into 8th, 7th and 6th *kyus* you will be expected to have added more difficult moves to your repertoire, such as the side kick and round-house kick, and be performing more complex *katas*.

However, at this level you will continue to be judged mainly on your balance, control and coordination. It's when you have progressed to 5th *kyu* and above that you will be expected to know what to do and, at gradings, will be marked on your increasing speed, power and reflexes. It's at this point that sparring at the gradings becomes more important.

At black belt level and above (1st to 10th *dan*), how you perform basic techniques is still vital to your progression, but emphasis will be placed on how you use them in combination and sparring situations. It's worth noting that passing your 1st *dan* black belt does not mean you have finished learning, as there are as many grades to progress through after that as there were before it.

Level	Colour of belt	Grade
10th *kyu*	white belt	beginner
9th *kyu*	red belt	basic punches and blocks; front and back stance; *kata* incorporating those techniques
8th *kyu*	yellow belt	adding front kicks to your repertoire
7th *kyu*	orange belt	adding riding stance and side kicks
6th *kyu*	green belt	adding block/punch combinations; light, controlled sparring
5th *kyu*	blue belt	adding block/kick and kick/punch combinations
4th *kyu*	purple belt	as above but now with emphasis on speed, power and reflexes. You should be performing with increased skill and confidence
3rd *kyu*	brown belt	once you have reached brown belt level it is a matter of constantly improving what you have already learnt – free sparring will be required and *katas* will be complicated
2nd *kyu*	brown belt	(second degree)
1st *kyu*	brown belt	(third degree)
1st–10th *dan*	black belts	the *katas* and approaches to combinations will become increasingly complex, plus, at this level, great emphasis will be placed on your attitude to karate, training and the *dojo*, as you are now a senior student

Moving on up

To advance through the belts will be every *karateka*'s goal, but that is only peripheral to how you are learning and progressing. Improving your karate is about much more than successful gradings.

Work hard

As we said in the previous pages, everybody's progress is individual and students of a similar rank will not be expected to do exactly the same things at the same levels of proficiency. Therefore, the best recipe for progression is to try your best at all times, and to remember you will be constantly assessed by your instructor as to whether you are ready to take the next grading or not. And this evaluation will be based on much more than how well you can execute your style's blocks, kicks and punches; how you approach training, your fellow students and the *dojo* itself will figure highly in these assessments, and age, too, will be taken into account. So it can't be overstressed that there are very few hiding places in the *dojo*, and if you are not making the effort you will soon be found out. In karate, more so than in many other sports, what you will get back is in direct proportion to what you put in.

It should take at least three months of regular training – at least three one-hour sessions per week – before a total beginner will be ready for their first grading. These initial classes will concentrate on stances, straightforward blocks and punches and the basic front kick, but much work will need to be done on most beginners' flexibility and fitness. There should be a basic *kata* learnt at this point to teach you how to start putting moves together in sequences. Many clubs will take longer on this initial stage and you may not take your 9th *kyu* for up to six months; this is because they will believe that this grounding is the most important part of your karate training. However, an equal number will try to award students a coloured belt as quickly as possible in order to encourage them to continue. Neither way of doing things is right or wrong, as long as both make sure you have the best grounding possible as you prepare to move up the ranks. However, if you feel you are being rushed into taking gradings then you probably are.

As you progress up the ranks, you should increase your training schedule, with sessions either becoming longer or more frequent or both. This is because beginners' sessions are often cut short due to the students' initial fitness and having so much to absorb. Many clubs operate a policy with beginners that will only teach three new things at a time, in order for the student to fully take them in before trying to learn something else.

Don't worry about a slow start though. Once you understand the basics of karate, it is much easier to take increasing amounts of new information on board and your progress will seem to gain pace. If you train hard for two or three two-hour sessions a week, you should be taking a grading every four to six months, and get to black belt standard in between three and four years. Some clubs will insist you enter tournaments as part of your gradings assessments.

As you will find out, the best things about learning karate is you get back exactly what you put in.

want to know more?
• Joining a karate club will be your next logical step. There are many clubs either run by local authorities or on local authority premises and a list of them should be available from your council's sport and leisure department.
• See page 178 for what to look for when choosing a karate club.
• If you want to buy karate equipment, a *gi*, body protection for sparring or a sparring aid such as a punchbag or a makiwara (see page 111), it's best to go to a specialist karate shop.

weblink
www.sportfocus.com has a comprehensive list of karate equipment retailers.

Glossary

Below is a list of the Japanese terms used in the basic study of karate and within this book. There are many, many more that you will learn as you progress as a *karateka*.

Age: upper, upwards or rising
Age-gyaki-zuki: upper reverse punch
Age oi-zuki: upper lunge punch
Age-uke: rising block
Age-zuki: upwards punch

Bunkai: the application of karate moves without an opponent, i.e. as part of a *kata*

Chudan: middle
Chudan-zuki: middle punch

Dachi: stance – it will usually have a prefix determining which stance
Dan: black belt ranking
Dojo: formal karate training hall, or, literally, 'the place of the Way'

Empi: elbow
Empi-uchi: elbow strike

Gedan: lower or downwards
Gedan-gyaki-zuke: lower reverse punch
Gedan-oi-zuki: lower lunge punch
Gedan-uke: downwards block
Gedan-zuki: low punch
Geri-keage: snap kick
Geri-kekomi: thrust kick

Gi: karate suit
Gyaki-zuki: reverse punch

Hachiji-dachi: natural stance – feet shoulder width apart, pointing at 45-degree angle
Hajime: begin (command for sparring or *kata*)
Hansoku: foul (called during sparring)
Heisoku-dachi: informal attention stance
Hidari: left
Hittsui: knee

Ippon: one point (as called in sparring)

Jiyu-kumite: free sparring
Jodan: upper, rising or head area
Jodan-age-uke: rising block
Jodan-kekomi: head high thrust kick
Jodan-mae-geri: high front kick
Jodan-zuki: high punch
Juji-uke: X block

Kamae-te: assume fighting stance
Karate: empty hand
Karateka: student/practitioner of karate
Kata: form – sequence of karate movements without an opponent

Keri: kick

Kiai: the yell given when a movement is completed, releasing inner energy and spirit

Kiba-dachi: riding stance (sometimes called horse stance or straddle stance)

Kokutsu-dachi: back stance

Kyu: the colours, or the belts below black

Mae-geri: front kick

Mae-geri-keage: front snap kick

Mae-geri-kekomi: front thrust kick

Makiwara: Resistance equipment. Originated in Okinawa at the same time as karate itself was developing. A good makiwara was 'tuned', with the tapering gauged to give it a flexibility that would flex (but with some resistance) when a strike landed correctly, but a badly struck blow would leave it rigid and jolt the puncher's arm. (See also page 111)

Mawashi-geri: roundhouse kick

Migi: right

Modotte: return to original position (a sparring command)

Naore: return to *Heisoku-dachi* (informal attention stance), the command usually given at the end of an exercise of *kata*

Rei: bow

Sayuzuki: double strike

Seiza: sit

Sensei: teacher or instructor

Shuto: knife hand

Shuto-uchi: knife hand strike

Shuto-uke: knife hand block

Soto: outwards

Soto-uke: outside block

Tai sabaki: evasive body movement

Uchi: strike

Uchi-uke: inwards block

Ude: forearm

Uke: block

Urakeen: back fist

Ushiro-geri: back kick

Wazari: one half-point (in sparring)

Yame: stop

Yoi: begin

Yoko: side

Yoko-geri-keage: side snap kick

Yoko-geri-kekomi: side thrust kick

Zenkutsu-dachi: front stance

Zuki: punch (pronounced tzuki)

Need to know more?

Organizations

British Institute of Karate Organization
www.bik.org.uk
A countrywide membership of clubs, the BIKO acknowledges a wide variety of styles.

British Karate Association
www.britishkarateassociation.co.uk
The long-standing BKA has a long list of associated clubs.

British Traditional Karate Association
http://btka.org.uk
Specialising in Washinkai, a style derived from Wado-ryu.

Byakko Shotokan Karate Association
www.byakko.co.uk
Yorkshire-based organization; regularly brings in international Shotokan superstars for exhibition and instruction (Byakko translates as 'white tiger').

English Contact Karate Association
www.ecka.co.uk
Uses full safety equipment during sparring, as students practise realistic combat.

English Karate Organisation
www.eko.me.uk
Affiliated to the European Karate Association.

English Shotokan Academy
www.the-esa.co.uk
Midlands-located, very traditional in its approach to Shotokan.

European Karate Organization Kyokushinkaikan
www.eko.org.uk
Branches all across the continent and in the UK.

Federation of English Karate Organisations International
www.feko.co.uk
Associated with Karate England, it has 73 member associations around the country.

Karate England (2005) Ltd
www.karateengland.org.uk
Based at the Bisham Abbey National Sports Centre. Their website has a directory of UK karate associations and federations.

Karate-London
www.karate-london.co.uk
Part of Shotokan Karate England, they
offer classes in North London and the
surrounding areas.

Karate Union of Great Britain
www.kugb.org
There are over 400 Shotokan clubs on the
KUGB's register.

Shotokan Karate
www.shotokankarate.org.uk
An affiliation of clubs and *dojos* in the
Midlands, teaching very traditional
Shotokan karate.

Shotokan Traditional Karate
Organisation (UK)
http://shoto.org
A series of *dojos* in the North London
area, teaching traditional Shotokan
karate.

United Kingdom All Styles Karate
Organisation
www.ukasko.com
The UKASKO has a huge database of
affiliated clubs.

Welsh Shotokan Karate
Organisation
www.wsko.org
Karate clubs in Wales.

The Competition Karate Association
www.cka.org.uk
An organization dedicated to British
karate competitions, explaining what
goes on in the different styles, what the
rules are, the history of karate and giving
guidelines for free sparring.

World Seido Karate Organization
http://seido.org.uk
There are seven clubs in the UK for this
relatively new style.

Useful Websites
DMOZ Open Directory
www.dmoz.org/Sports/Martial_Arts/
Organisations
A continually updated directory listing
clubs and organizations in the UK and
abroad.

SportFocus
www.sportfocus.com
The karate section of this all-sport
website lists clubs, association, leagues
and equipment retailers.

Further reading

Karate-Do Nyumon: The Master Introductory Text

Gichin Funakoshi

(Oxford University Press)

Before his death in 1957, Master Funakoshi (founder of the Shotokan style) sought to demystify karate, and open it up to as many people as possible. This book is a collection of his previously unpublished writings and some *katas*.

25 Shoto-kan Katas

Shojiro Sugiyama

(Shojiro Sugiyama)

Not only does this book clearly explain the *katas'* movements with drawings and photographs as well as description, it also delves into the philosophy behind them. Its aim, as with all Sugiyama's teachings, is to promote a complete understanding of the art.

Dynamic Karate (Bushido – The Way of The Warrior)

Masatoshi Nakayama

(Oxford University Press)

In great detail and with as much attention to the 'why' as the 'what', this book distils karate's fundamentals so as to rebuild technique with power and directness to achieve maximum impact. A book for experienced *karateka* as much as the beginner.

Essentials of Wado-ryu Karate

Chris Thompson

(Paul H. Crompton Ltd)

Clear illustrations and explanations of the style's basic techniques, with fascinating context provided by the history and significance of Wado-ryu.

Karate Basics

Robin Rielly

(Tuttle Publishing)

Contains a comprehensive and fascinating history of karate, and provides a great deal of insight into the theories and spirituality of the martial arts movements.

DVD
Winning Competition Karate

Tsunami Productions

A slick presentation, explaining and demonstrating the moves and counter-moves that will get you ahead on the mat. However, this is not for complete beginners as the level of instruction requires a degree of prior knowledge.

Acknowledgements

The author would like to express his gratitude to Tyrone Whyte and his karate club in Stratford, East London, without whose energy and cheerful co-operation there would be very few photographs in this book.

Sensai Tyrone Whyte (pictured below, front row centre) is a 6th *dan* black belt, and a former English, British and European Kumite champion. He specialises in tournament *karate do* and traditional karate, comprising *ky kushin-kai* basics and *Ishin-ryu* fighting style. In his club, students must compete in tournaments as part of their advancement through the grades.

The students who took part in the photography sessions are: Norman Clark, Martin Clark, Joe Simpson, Ciaran Dempsey, Daniel Browne, Angelo Agathangelou and Pauline Morgan.

Index

☾ Collins need to know?

Look out for these recent titles in Collins' practical and accessible need to know? series.

Other titles in the series:

Antique Marks
Aquarium Fish
Birdwatching
Body Language
Buying Property in France
Buying Property in Spain
Card Games
Card Making
Chess
Children's Parties
Codes & Ciphers
Decorating
Digital Photography
DIY
Dog Training
Drawing & Sketching
Dreams

First Aid
Golf
Guitar
How to Lose Weight
Kama Sutra
Kings and Queens
Knots
Low GI/GL Diet
Mushroom Hunting
NLP
Outdoor Survival
Party Games
Pilates
Poker
Pregnancy
Property
Speak French

Speak Italian
Speak Spanish
Stargazing
Watercolour
Weather Watching
Weddings
Wine
Woodworking
The World
Universe
Yoga
Zodiac Types

To order any of these titles, please telephone 0870 787 1732 quoting reference 263H. For further information about all Collins books, visit our website: www.collins.co.uk